Alpine Hunting in New Zealand

Alpine Hunting in New Zealand

Roger Lentle and Frank Saxton

David Bateman

Dedication
For William Harvey and Mark Saxton

*Home is the hunter,
home from the hill*

Acknowledgements
Thanks to
Graham Henry, Dr John Parke and Hamish Barham.

Authors' note

In the context of this book the name "tahr" refers only to the Himalayan tahr *(Hemitragus jemlahicus)*. There are in fact three species of tahr, the others being Nilgiri tahr *(Hemitragus hylocrius)* and the Arabian tahr *(Hemitragus jayakari)*. The word tahr is sometimes spelt thar, but the leading expert, George Schaller, considers this to be a misspelling.

By the same authors
Red Deer in New Zealand: A complete hunting manual (Bateman, 1991)
Stalking the Seasons Round: A year-round guide to hunting deer in New Zealand (Bateman, 1993)

First published in 1994 by David Bateman Ltd., "Golden Heights", 32-34 View Road, Glenfield, Auckland 10, New Zealand.

Copyright © Roger Lentle and Frank Saxton, 1994
Copyright © David Bateman Ltd., 1994

This book is copyright. Except for the purpose of fair review, no part may be stored or transmitted by any means, electronic or mechanical, including recording or storage in any information retrieval system, without permission in writing from the publisher. No reproduction may be made, whether by photocopying or by any other means, unless a license has been obtained from the publisher or its agent.

ISBN 1 86953 173 6

Line illustrations by Ray Burns
Pointillism illustrations and photographs by Lance Barnard
Typesetting and jacket design by Chris O'Brien/Pages Literary Pursuits
Printed in Hong Kong by Colorcraft

Contents

Introduction *6*
1 The mountains and mountain skills *10*
2 Equipment for alpine hunting *33*
3 Hunting chamois *48*
4 Hunting tahr *82*
5 Deer in the mountains *106*
Appendix 1: Examining horns to find the best areas for trophy hunting *115*
Appendix 2: Ballistics for alpine hunters *118*
Appendix 3: Wind chill *122*
Appendix 4: Chamois usage of alpine zones *123*
Glossary *124*
Bibliography *129*
Index *131*

Introduction

For many New Zealand big-game hunters a goodly portion of the lure of the sport is the experience of being out and about in wild and beautiful places. In alpine hunting, the toughest of New Zealand hunting sports, the quality of the scenic experience rises to the spectacular. The sheer exhilaration of hunting against such a scenic backdrop is surely part of the reason for its popularity.

Alpine hunting (the sport of hunting above the bush-line) is, however, a demanding speciality. There is the challenge of combining mountaineering skills with hunting an elusive and fleet-footed quarry. A high degree of fitness and marksmanship at distance is required, to say nothing of sheer dogged determination. In spite of this, or perhaps in part because of it, there is no shortage of recruits eager to secure a trophy chamois or tahr head as well as enjoy the mountain hunting experience.

Surprisingly, there has not so far been available a New Zealand book that draws together the facts needed by alpine hunters. This book sets out to remedy this situation. The reader will find detailed information on the habits and haunts of chamois and tahr, presented in the same style as our previous two books *Red Deer in New Zealand* and *Stalking the Seasons Round*. We also discuss hunting red deer and wapiti, as these emerge at times onto the high tops.

There is also a chapter on the mountaineering skills needed by alpine hunters, and another on specialized alpine hunting equipment. This is vital for the beginner alpine hunter, and for this reason is dealt with first.

For the experienced hunter, we include not only the latest scientific information on the quarry but also a number of more advanced practical considerations which may increase your enjoyment of the

Introduction

sport. For example, in Appendix 1 a system for identifying potential trophy areas is described.

A final point addressed to the beginner: While the information in this book will give you the required factual knowledge to enable you to take up the sport, it is still no substitute for hands-on experience. Before you go alpine hunting on your own, especially in winter, ***you must gain experience in the company of qualified mountaineering instructors and with veteran alpine hunters.***

Mountains, mountain skills and equipment

Hardships?
Let me tell you about hardships!
motto of the London Explorers' Club

1
The mountains and mountain skills

We had started out from Fairlie at 5 a.m. on a winter's morning while it was still dark. Morning broke while we were speeding along the Lochaber road but there was little to show for it. The thick mist enveloping the little rag-top Landrover took on a faint rosy tinge but the gloom of night persisted. Riding as passenger, it was my duty to bail out at the numerous gates, open and then close them after the vehicle had driven through. I noticed as I shivered at the gate to Lochaber Station that the entire ragtop was highlighted in hoar frost, and thought God help us if we stall in the river on a morning like this.

Half an hour later as the little Series Two heaved itself dripping like a wet dog from the river in question I sighed with relief and moved on to the next worry, 'would the cloud lift?' This question was not to be answered until two hours later. Having parked the transport and trudged 500 metres up a tussock-clad spur, we emerged, crusted like the truck with hoar, above the cloud into a brilliant morning of blue sky and hot sun on purple mists below.

Our destination was a series of rocky bluffs now visible far above, the rock faces dark in between generous burdens of snow. As we climbed, the crisp covering of well-frosted snow deepened until at last, a scant hundred feet beneath the bluffs, it became an even blanket disguising the bulging forms of the snow tussocks.

We worked to windward of the rock formation above us, gradually climbing out onto a thin ridge that led to the upper brim of a cliff. Finally we reached the brim, emerging onto the very spine of a steep mountain range that fell sharply away on both sides. A pause to catch our breath, stamp the snow from our well-nailed boots, and the hunt was on.

The mountains and mountain skills

Somewhere in the jumbled rock architecture of the cliff side beneath us was a herd of tahr. Bob, the Lochaber Station member of our party, had seen them here just a few weeks before while mustering. We glassed down from our lofty perch searching the crannies of the rock gully beneath our feet. The trouble was, the snow cornice on which we now stood was so built up that it prevented us from getting a good view of the rocks immediately below us. To do so would have meant venturing out to the very rim of the cornice. Instead we had to content ourselves with glassing obliquely down the walls of the rock buttresses that jutted well out from the face. Even then we had a poor view and saw no tracks or animals. There was nothing for it but to work our way along the crest of the range above the cliffs and try to find a place with a better downward view.

Here we struck another problem — or at least I should say that I thought it a problem, although Bob did not. So steep was the spine of the ridge on which we were perched that there was no route along the top of the pinnacles of rock that projected upwards from its leading edge. Instead we would have to work our way across the cornices of snow that were stuck to their sides. The prospect was, to me at least, fearful, for in places the cornices had broken off, avalanching away to leave only a thin rim of the upper edge plastered onto the rock wall, looking somewhat like a bracket fungus sticking to the side of a tree.

However, I was in the minority. Bob was quite nonchalant about it, and Alan, the other member of the party, was a seasoned mountaineer and therefore similarly unconcerned. I took the rear, being careful to follow on the inner side of the footprints left by my companions. I found myself torn between two opposing hazards. On the one hand the slope of the cornice was steep, forcing me to stamp in each foot as I progressed in order to keep from sliding over the edge of the cornice and into oblivion. On the other, I was acutely aware that each stamp could unstick the slab of cornice and send it and me plummeting to the rocks below.

Needless to say we progressed slowly, but by late morning had crossed eight such hazards and obtained a series of views of the cliff below that were in hunting terms unrewarding.

Lunchtime brought new setbacks. My mate Alan, instead of attacking the sandwiches with his usual gusto, announced that he was sick and feeling worse by the minute. Indeed, he looked white and sweaty enough to convince Bob and me that a quick return homeward from the mountain eyrie was definitely in order. After hastily packing up the lunchtime goodies and returning to the first corniced area we discovered the warm sunlight had softened the snow. We found this out when Bob, in attempting to cross, sank up to his knees in soft snow. He started to run, and just got clear before the whole lot went roaring over the cliff edge below. At this point I became heartily glad that we had had the foresight to bring a climbing rope.

Five hours later we reached the ridge we had so eagerly ascended that morning, and started a slushy and dispirited descent to the Landrover, the mountain announcing its victory behind us in a series of echoing snow-slab falls.

As we descended Alan's sickness wore off, and by the time we reached the level where tussocks were showing through the snow, he spotted a group of tahr feeding below us, a mile or so upwind. They at least had had enough sense to avoid the snowy heights on a warm sunny day. It was difficult to carry out the 'softly, softly' Red Indian-style approach with the mountains' intermittent thunder making the beasts jittery, but we managed it and Alan got an acceptable trophy.

We returned to the vehicle well after dark and reached the station homestead just in time to see the manager starting to worry, but it was nothing that a bottle of Famous Grouse (specially carried for such emergencies) couldn't fix. I made a mental resolve to study the subject of mountaineering a little harder. RL

Introduction

The typical New Zealand big-game hunter starts the long apprenticeship in the art of hunting by stalking red deer, usually at first in the river flats and bush terraces. Here, he or she discovers the ways of the quarry, and at the same time develops a knowledge of, and empathy with, the mountains. This knowledge grows stronger with each successive expedition.

Sooner or later, however, the hunter will emerge into the alpine world of tussock, rock and ice. At first this is a temporary emergence as the seasonal shifts of the quarry are followed: perhaps the late spring wanderings of red stags in velvet, or even the autumn bugling of Fiordland wapiti acting as a summons to these remote places. In some hunters, a temptation to linger and to become a specialist alpine hunter is kindled.

For apart from the ethereal beauty of the mountain tops, there are other new experiences to beckon the hunter/mountaineer. The high places are the home of two hitherto unfamiliar game species — the chamois and the tahr. Such hardy beasts are seldom dwellers on the lower forest slopes, utilizing only its upper fringe. These animals prefer steep-walled alpine chasms which are often coated with snow or ice. They live here through all seasons, offering year-round sport to those who would hunt them.

But the hunter drawn by such attractions needs first to learn to go safely in this new world. What, on a fine day, can seem an innocent and beautiful place, may have many traps for the unwary. So it is here we will start, with the mountains and their dangers. First we will discuss how to go about the business of alpine hunting with the minimum of risk, and only then move to the habits of the hunter's new-found alpine quarry. A recent incident in the Southern Alps illustrates the value of learning alpine hunting in this order.

Two alpine-equipped hunters arrived at a hut, only to find it was already being used by two other hunters equipped more in the style of Barry Crump's Good Keen Man: lace-up gumboots, shorts, swanndri and a complete absence of snow gear. These hut residents were full of good-humoured jokes at the expense of the more 'dandified' arrivals with their brightly-coloured alpine clothing, ice axes, crampons and other paraphernalia. The two parties agreed to hunt separate areas that afternoon. It was spring time, and the weather was fine and clear.

The alpine-equipped party had chosen a more distant hunting ground but failed to find any game. Returning to the hut at last light they anticipated more jokes about their 'unnecessary' gear, especially as they had heard shots from where the others had gone. However, they had the hut to themselves and it stayed that way all night. On waking, late, they cooked a large breakfast to see them through what looked like being a long day, and were about to leave on a search mission when the 'good keen men' returned, tired and bedraggled.

Their story was as follows. After leaving the hut they had made excellent time through the wet snow conditions created by the warm spring day. They were fit, and easily climbed a steep tussock slope that ran alongside a bluff system. On reaching the upper rim of the bluff they saw above them five chamois feeding on a steep face in a place where wet snow had slipped to expose the underlying tussock. The chamois soon spotted the hunters, but a barrage of enthusiastic shots produced the happy result of two dead bucks lying on the mountainside some 300 metres distant and above. It took time to climb up to the fallen beasts, skin them and take photos, and by then the sun was quickly slipping below the horizon. However the hunters were experienced bushmen, well used to travelling in the dark, and had good torches with them.

The descent from the fellfields was slow and by the time they reached the steeper slopes adjacent to the side of the bluff it was nearly dark. These slopes had been easy to scale earlier in the day, but the layer of sun-induced slush there had now frozen solid. From here down, the mountainside now presented an entirely different proposition for climbers in rubber boots, without even an ice axe. A short attempt to descend soon resulted in a fearful return to the relative safety of a small area of level ground. Here they spent the night, waiting and walking in circles just to keep warm. In the morning, by sheer good fortune, a clear sunrise produced a welcome return of warmth, re-melting the frozen crust and allowing them to return. **RL**

To hunt the alps, especially if you hunt in the colder months of the year, you need to become a competent mountaineer. Only by developing an understanding of the mountains will you be able to anticipate the more sinister hidden hazards. For example, any mountaineer will know just how lucky the 'good keen men' were in the story above. There were plenty of other problems beside those they did encounter. For example, they had climbed a wet snow slope on a warm spring day. In these conditions, steep snowy slopes often produce wet-snow avalanches. Not only this, but the position above the bluffs from where they shot the chamois was doubly dangerous as even a small avalanche coming off the slopes above could have swept them over the bluff edge to their deaths. All this is to say nothing of exposure to the elements. A storm that night could well have resulted in their deaths by hypothermia.

This book is, however, not intended to be one of basic mountaincraft. Nevertheless, we want at least to point out some of the hazards the alpine hunter is likely to encounter. Before embarking upon this we wish to stress again: **there is no substitute for proper training followed by practical experience of travelling in alpine country.**

A warning

Nothing can prepare you, if you have not experienced it before, to cope with a fall on an icy slope — even a slope with a relatively gentle incline. In an instant you are completely out of control, and you will not stop until the bottom. On the way down you may crash into obstacles, tumble many times head-over-heels, fall over a bluff... the possibilities are horrendous and very likely to be fatal.

This is just one example of the hazards that may await the unwary alpine hunter. **Unless you are already an experienced mountaineer, we strongly advise you to take a course in snow and ice technique, snowcraft and mountain safety.** Courses are run by mountaineering clubs, some tramping clubs and alpine guide companies in both the North and South Islands. They are inexpensive and well taught. You will probably enjoy yourself and may even take up mountaineering as a new sport. The experience will add immeasurably to your safety and confidence as an alpine hunter.

Trying to learn these things as you go along will only expose you to the kind of danger where your first mistake could be your last. You cannot expect to teach yourself the proper use of an ice axe, crampons, etc., any more than you can get behind the wheel of a car for the first time and drive safely.

More than this, when you have completed a course of instruction we advise you always to go in the company of experienced alpine hunters. After all, if you have learned the skills to stay out of trouble — and to cope with an emergency — shouldn't you expect your mates to be able to do the same too?

Avalanche

Alpine hunting often puts you at particular risk from avalanche. American research, for example, shows that avalanches are commonest on slopes of around 45 degrees — the very same slopes where tahr and chamois are often found in winter. This is no coincidence; the beasts simply choose areas where snow cover is more readily shed to expose the underlying grazing. Also, hunters often try to avoid the climbing difficulties of steep rocky places by ascending narrow valleys and guts, but in fact these are very prone to avalanche. Furthermore, much hunting is done on the lower portions of basins and bluff systems. When hunting in these areas, hunters are often oblivious to dangers from higher ground. All these are areas which mountaineers particularly try to avoid as they are too risky. So the alpine hunter needs to be, if anything, more of an avalanche expert than an ordinary mountaineer.

Snow deposition

Understanding how snow is laid down on a mountain is the first step in avalanche prediction.

When there is no wind, snow will fall straight down and land as a uniform blanket over everything. Such conditions, however, are rare in the mountains. More commonly there is a wind. In New Zealand the snow-bearing winds are usually southerly. Imagine a snow-filled southerly whipping along sideways into a mountain. As it approaches the south-facing side of the mountain, snow is thrown onto these slopes. Nearer the top of the mountain, however, the wind is deflected upwards and accelerates as it travels up and over the range. This deflected wind will often pick up snow from the upper south-facing slopes and deposit it not only on the lip of the ridge (forming a snow cornice), but also on the north-facing side when it slows down and drops its load. In these conditions heavy snow build-up occurs on the upper reaches of slopes that face *away* from the snow-bearing wind.

In strong wind conditions, the snow covering on the windward side of a range can be reduced to a thin layer, while on the lee side heavy drifts accumulate. On uneven mountainsides with hummocks, ridges and boulders, there will form a patchwork of deep snow areas on the lee sides and shallow snow on the windward sides of anything that obstructs the wind's flow.

To the animals that live above the snow-line, these conditions bring problems. Fur-bearing animals avoid strong, cold winds, tending to shelter in the lee of rocks and ridges. However, in snowdrift conditions, as we have seen, these are the very places where heavy snow build-up occurs. Thus, in such conditions even the most hardy beasts will be driven down-slope to areas where wind velocity is reduced. Here they will wait out the storm, sometimes then returning to graze on the windward slopes where the snow is thinner.

On sunny days in autumn, more snow melts on the north than the south-facing slopes. Nevertheless, as winter wears on the snow will gradually build in north-facing basins, guts and slopes that are sheltered from the prevailing wind. It is these accumulations that are the parents of avalanches. Thus we come to our first general rule: avalanches are more likely in areas where high snow build-up occurs, and this often means areas that are sheltered from the southerly wind.

After a heavy snowstorm, an avalanche is more likely. This is particularly so in areas where the slope is around 45 degrees, but it also happens on much gentler slopes. So, after a large snowfall you should

Fig. 1: Dry powder snow avalanche in mid flight. From Perla and Martinelli (1976), Avalanche Handbook.

be particularly alert, and avoid avalanche-prone areas as described above. 'Sluffs' — scars left on the surface of the snow by miniature avalanches of loose snow (see Fig. 2) — are a particular warning sign of avalanche danger. Sluffs occur high up on steep slopes and can be spotted at a distance through binoculars. Although they may be far above you, they often indicate greater risk of avalanche lower down.

Types of snow avalanche

While a sluff is a mini-avalanche of loose powder snow, avalanches of loose snow can occur on a larger scale and often reach massive proportions. These are called *powder-snow avalanches*. They are particularly likely just after a heavy snowfall, especially when the snow that has fallen is composed of a particular type of snowflake. A single type of snowflake shape may predominate in a snowstorm, and flakes with the familiar large, well-branched crystal structure often lock together as they settle on the mountainside so the snow is more stable. But if large, well-rounded flakes that resemble hailstones (sometimes called 'graupel') are formed, they fail to interlock and indeed are able to

Alpine Hunting in New Zealand

roll over each other. Powder-snow avalanches are the likely result.

An alpine hunter can build up experience of the types of snowflakes by examining the snow during and after a storm. Even if you cannot distinguish the physical shape of the flakes, you may be able to get an idea of whether the individual grains clump together readily or are prone to roll over each other, providing a danger warning.

Avalanches from fresh snow are relatively easy to predict, but unfortunately they are not the most common type the hunter will encounter. Much more frequent and dangerous are the avalanches caused by slippage of older snow. There are two types.

Wet-snow avalanches are perhaps the next most easy to predict as they only occur where the snow contains a lot of water. You can learn to recognize this condition simply by squeezing handfuls of

Fig. 2: Small, loose snow avalanches called 'sluffs' can give the hunter a clue that avalanches are likely. From Perla and Martinelli (1976), Avalanche Handbook.

snow and seeing if water comes out. Wet-snow avalanches are more likely in spring and summer, when snow-melt is underway, and are often triggered by a rainstorm which adds extra water. This water is important in causing these avalanches because it acts as a lubricant. In fact, a wet-snow avalanche behaves almost like a surge of water, but when it stops it re-freezes. Death comes quickly to anyone caught in this type of flow.

In a bluff system where several small chutes or watercourses feed into a large one, the danger is particularly great. This is because every time any snow from one of the little catchments above breaks away and feeds into the bigger catchment, it is liable to trigger off a more general avalanche. In this way the larger valley becomes a regular avalanche chute. It cannot be overstressed just how far down these deadly cascades of ice are able to reach: even places where these mobile snow-packs are completely out of sight. Would-be rescuers are themselves also at risk. Never venture into the 'rifle barrel' of a gut when there may be a high snow load above; for example during melt conditions, in rain, or if there are signs of recent avalanche debris. When hunting the lower slopes in spring and autumn, wait for clear frosty days and stick to ridgelines, preferring ridges that have a low snow load.

Always consider what is going on in the snowfields above you. If in doubt about an area, climb a safe ridge on the opposite side of the valley and glass the guts. Ribbons of dirty snow chunks (as well as sluffs) can indicate avalanche hazard.

Slab avalanches are possibly the most difficult to predict, and are common in New Zealand. In this type of avalanche, a slab or layer of snow comes loose and skids down the mountain, often churning itself into fine powder as it goes. Even a small slab is dangerous. Slab avalanches have various causes, basically from a layer of one type of snow overtopping another and the two not bonding together. There are both soft and hard slab avalanches, the former where blown snow has been deposited as the upper layer, and the latter where the upper snow layer has been suddenly compacted (often by wind). Avalanche prediction work is done routinely on ski-fields and near the Homer Tunnel, so if hunting near these you could ask for slab-avalanche forecasts. Elsewhere, the following suggestions may help.

Sometimes a slab avalanche will, like a powder avalanche, occur soon after a heavy snowfall. It is thought that this results from a change of conditions *during* the snowstorm. This change causes either

Alpine Hunting in New Zealand

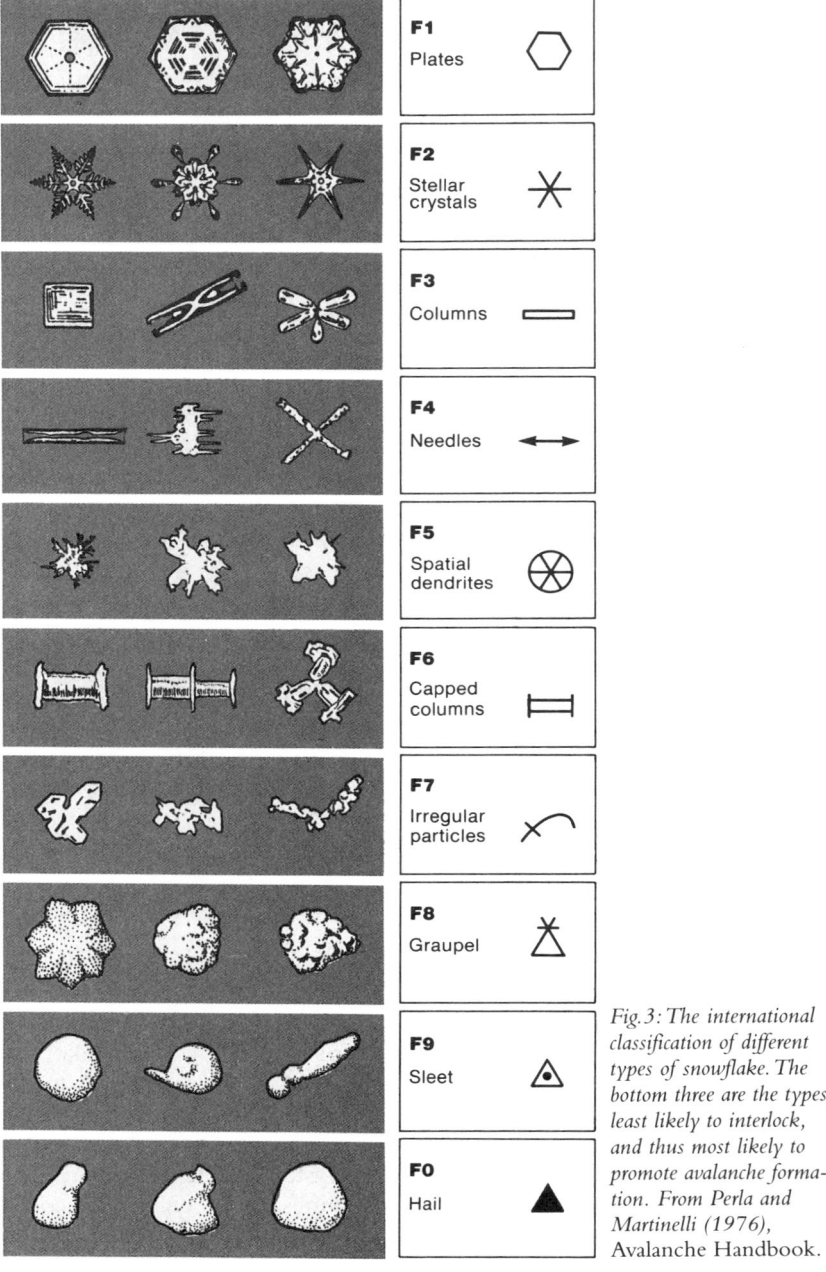

Fig.3: The international classification of different types of snowflake. The bottom three are the types least likely to interlock, and thus most likely to promote avalanche formation. From Perla and Martinelli (1976), Avalanche Handbook.

a gradual change in shape of the snowflakes between the start and finish of the snowfall, or a change in the density of packing of the snow. In either case, a weak layer develops under denser snow. This built-in fault later causes the slab to detach itself from the rest. Conditions which can give rise to this situation are:

1. A storm that starts off cold and then becomes warmer. (Conversely, a falling temperature during a storm is thought to yield more a stable snow-pack.)
2. A storm that starts with a significant period of light winds followed by a period of stronger winds.
3. Either of the above, coupled with a change in the type of snowflake from light and flaky to a heavy, rounded type.

Apart from these causes of slab avalanche, there is a more sneaky one. This again comes about when a weak layer of snow forms under the part that detaches, but in this case it is caused by a change in grain size of the snowflakes as they lie within the snow-pack. Two situations can bring this about. Firstly, when the surface layers of the snow become cooler than those below. This is particularly likely with thin snow in clear weather, and causes a change in crystal structure that makes the snow more slippery underneath. Secondly, in another, slightly different process, large 'slippery crystals' can form when the snow partially thaws and then re-freezes. So be mindful of the hazards of slab avalanche during or after a run of clear sunny days or frosty nights in spring or autumn, when snow cover is likely to be thin.

Sometimes you will encounter a snow edge on a face or bluff in which you can see a distinct layer of large (up to 4 mm) snow crystals with denser snow overlying. Then proceed carefully, as you are likely to be in a hazardous area. An even more ominous sign is a distinct crunching sound beneath your feet as you walk. This is caused by the weaker layer in the snow giving way. If visible cracks also form, even novices will realise that they are in the centre of an area that is about to slip (see Fig. 5). The problem is what to do next! The recommended drill is as follows.

If caught in an avalanche
First, take off your pack, unsling your rifle and hold them in your hands. This will enable you to drop them instantly, if necessary, to lighten your weight. If only small cracks are forming around your

Fig. 4: Examples of slab avalanche fracture patterns. From Perla and Martinelli (1976), Avalanche Handbook.

feet you may be able to get away with still hanging onto your load and quickly and carefully going *straight up* out of the area. If the cracks start to radiate further and further away from you, at once drop your load in the snow (you can always buy a new pack and rifle) before moving up. By going straight up you are less likely to create further lines of weakness in the snow slab with your footfalls. Horizontal steps across a convex snow face are like an invitation to 'tear off along the dotted line' as far as a slab avalanche is concerned. If the cracks really grow rapidly and the snow slabs start to move, it is useless to try to outrun the avalanche. If, however, a large rock or tree is near at hand, try and get yourself to it.

If you are carried off by an avalanche, instantly let go of anything you are carrying. Lie on your back, face upwards, and make backstroke-type arm movements in an effort to 'swim' on the surface of the snow, keeping your head uphill. If buried in the snow, try to hold your breath until the snow stops. Holding your breath in like this expands your ribcage and makes a slightly bigger space in the snow so you can breathe while waiting for rescue. Also, while being swept along by the avalanche, try to cup a hand over your mouth to create a breathing space. Hold the other hand and arm straight up. With a bit of luck, when you come to a halt it will stick out of the snow and give your mate your location.

If you are buried in an avalanche, it's often difficult to know which way up you are. The quick test is, if circumstances permit, to dribble! Saliva will unerringly obey gravity and show you which way is down.

Helping someone else caught in an avalanche
If it is your mate who is swept away, you have to move fast to get him or her out. If you lose sight of him, first search the area where he was when the avalanche started, secondly search the point on the mountainside where you lost sight of him, and lastly, if you can recognize it, the bit of the snow surface (which will have moved downhill) where you lost sight of him. You haven't got long. American data shows only a 40% survival rate after burial for more than an hour.

Avoiding avalanche areas
It is unlikely that the cautious hunter will get into the middle of a potential avalanche formation area, as game animals are as careful as humans to avoid these places. If you do get caught it is most likely to be in an avalanche that formed well above.

A well-churned-up slab avalanche can behave like a powder avalanche and cross gullies rather than flow in them, heading downhill by the shortest possible route. In this case, hunters on a spur may not be as safe as they are from wet snow avalanches. These avalanches tend to recur in the same places, even during the same season, and this fact can help you avoid them altogether. This is because a particular ground shape can cause tension lines in the snow-pack as it forms. For example, a bulge in the surface can cause a shear line to form in the snowfield at the same place year after year when the conditions are right. You can often identify such areas by keeping a lookout for damage from previous seasons, for example broken-off tree trunks or branches bearing long-dead leaves. The avalanche snow itself may have melted, but tell-tale debris persists.

Catabatic winds

Unlike avalanches, catabatic winds are not a danger. But they are often crucial to your alpine-hunting success, and failure to plan for them can ruin your efforts.

Catabatic (also spelt katabatic) winds arise from the combined effects of the heat of the sun and the cold of the ice and snow on the air in the mountains. On still nights in winter, heat radiates straight out into the vastness of space, so the high snow fields become extremely cold. As the air cools it becomes more dense and rolls down the mountain to create a down-valley wind — a catabatic wind. Next morning, if the clear conditions persist, the sun will warm rock-faces and even the surface of the snow. This heat is transmitted to the overlying air, making it expand and become less dense. It thus rises, drawing up more air to replace it from the valley below. So in the morning an up-slope, up-valley catabatic wind is formed. Similar winds can form even where there is cloud or when there is little snow. However, these are not so strong.

Consider the following typical alpine-hunting situation. You are hunting a set of bluffs for chamois but staying at a hut in the valley below. One strategy you could consider would be to get up early and climb up to the top of the ridge above the bluffs. While climbing, the

Fig. 5 (opposite): *A slab avalanche before and after. This unique series of pictures shows the whole process. A hunter would undoubtedly not escape easily and would have to adopt the avalanche survival procedure referred to in the text. From Perla and Martinelli (1976),* Avalanche Handbook.

wind would still be blowing downwards and any animals encountered would be up-wind above you. But by the time you have got up above the bluffs, the catabatic wind is likely to be ready to change into up-slope mode. You are now in an excellent position to hunt down the bluffs, on top of the chamois.

An alternative strategy would be to walk up the valley at first light, arriving at the foot of the bluffs while the wind is still blowing down-slope, and so hunt upwards below the animals. This has two disadvantages. Firstly, hunting upwards to chamois is less effective than hunting down towards them. Secondly, you will have less time to hunt before the wind changes. Once it changes it will carry your scent to any animals above you and up-valley from you. Your best option when caught in these conditions is to sidle back down-valley, slowly climbing the mountainside as you go. By doing this you will have the wind in your favour for any animals below and down-valley of you.

Falling rocks

Frost-heave is a process by which larger stones are brought to the surface by the action of frost. Ice crystals repeatedly forming and melting slowly push rocks up out of the soil. It is important to be aware of this because it causes one of the greatest alpine hazards — falling rocks. In the morning sun, the cement of frost that holds these surface rocks is loosened, causing them to fall. Even a small rock rapidly becomes a lethal projectile.

Falling rocks are a much bigger problem in summer than winter. In winter, more rocks are snow-buried and the temperature may stay below freezing all day so even exposed rocks won't loosen up. On a summer morning, even after a cold night a steady downward rain of rocks and stones is likely.

The danger is also very great in summer at high altitudes. During the day, melt-water seeps into cracks, then it freezes and expands during the night. This fractures the rock, and when the early sun strikes the slopes the rocks begin to fall. Therefore the most dangerous time of all is when the early morning sun plays on the slopes far above the hunter.

Falling rocks tend to follow rather haphazard trajectories, so the usual advice given is to wait until the last moment before leaping out of the way. But there may be lots of rocks coming down at once —

one falling rock tends to dislodge others — so the danger is best avoided altogether. It's safer to wait until afternoon or nearly evening. Alternatively, wait for cloudy conditions when this problem is not so bad. Again, on a clear frosty morning the hunter who climbs early and high, then hunts down, is in a safer position.

When winter is well advanced, frosts often penetrate deep into the ground, creating other hazards. The loose shingle fan that was easy and safe to run down in the summer can now become a frozen slide. The alpine hunter wanting an easy descent path may encounter little difficulty in the upper, sun-warmed parts, but strike big trouble lower down. Here, in the more shaded regions, the stones may have become welded together by frost and no longer slip away to provide a foothold. Worse, after a day's full sun the shingle fan can appear loose on the surface but consist of only a thin coat of mobile stones overlying a frozen core. A hunter venturing onto such a slope is liable to find himself catapulting downwards at a fearsome speed, and even if lucky enough to arrest his flight will have great difficulty climbing back up.

Cold

Wind chill
Hunters used to the lower slopes of mountains and the confines of forests often underestimate the chilling potential of the high alpine environment. The wind-chill chart (see Appendix 3) graphically illustrates what happens when cold and wind combine to assault an unprotected human being.

Hypothermia
A hunter exposed in a cold but not flesh-freezing wind can slip slowly into hypothermia. This is an extremely dangerous condition. All alpine hunters should know the signs of hypothermia, and how to treat it. These are well documented in even the most basic mountaineering and bushcraft books. Two good books are: *Mountaincraft; Mountain Safety Manual No.3* (ed. A. J. Heine) from the Mountain Safety Council of New Zealand and *Mountaineering: The Freedom of the Hills* (ed. P. Ferber).

Sudden storms
If caught out in a sudden storm there may be no alternative but to go

to ground. Alpine hunters should be familiar with the standard emergency-survival techniques such as building snow caves. This information is found in the basic mountaineering books referred to above, but is best learned by attending a mountaineering course where survival techniques are taught.

Creeping cold

This is a less dramatic but more common hazard. Poorly fitting boots or too many socks, for example, may merely produce painful friction blisters in a lowland deerstalker; but up in the alpine world, such incaution can easily result in frostbite. Both of us, at different times, have had frostbitten toes. In Frank's case it was caused by walking through a river and then spending six hours hunting in deep, soft snow. Frank's wet footwear allowed the cold to creep slowly through boots and socks to freeze his toes and the ball of one foot.

A good mountaineer pays as much subconscious attention to the sense of feeling in his extremities as a deerstalker does to the wind on his face and neck. Toes and fingers should be wiggled and worked at every pause to keep good circulation. Sometimes you may lose feeling in a particular part of your body, but moving it should restore the circulation. If this does not work and you can't get the feeling back quickly you should immediately retreat to shelter and warm the affected part with your hands or body; for example by putting cold fingers under warm armpits or onto your crutch. In the event that the chilling is too advanced for a quick on-the-job re-warming, it is likely to be better to retreat to base camp before thawing the affected part. This is firstly because considerable pain will come with the thawing, and secondly because the part should be rested and not used after the thawing. You will in this situation have sustained a deep-tissue frostbite — meaning an end to the trip and a few months before you will be mountain-fit again.

After I had moved to the North Island, the hunting trip that was on the top of my list of must-do's was a sortie after the wily sika. However, the Kaimanawas and Kawekas were a long way from Wellington — too far for a weekend trip, and the rigours of university duties plus a busy general practice precluded any longer spell away. It was a good two years before I found time for the trip. By then I had got to know a friendly neighbourhood mountaineer-cum-pharmacist by the name of Hamish Barham. He had hunted the Kawekas since his childhood and would be happy to take me on a first 'recce' trip after the sneaky sika.

The mountains and mountain skills

We set out on a Friday morning. I had been on call the night before and as usual was only half-organized, but at 7 a.m. we just grabbed everything, including my rather surprised Visla dog Wredd, threw it in the back of the Toyota, and ran. By midday we were nearing the little settlement of Puketitiri and made a break in our journey to pick up Hamish's hunting cobber, who was anxious to join in the fun. As I helped him load his gear in the back of my 4X4, I sized him up. Between them, these two North Island types were starting to get me worried. They were both two inches taller than me and looking a good deal fitter.

An hour later we parked up at the Makahu saddle road end and my worries multiplied a hundredfold. A first look at the height of the main Kawekas had confirmed that it was within my capabilities — but could I do it at these characters' pace? I quietly resolved not to be rushed, adhering to the proper tramping maxim of travelling at my own pace.

Then I discovered that in the rush to get away I had grabbed my daughter Tabitha's tramping boots instead of my own. Needless to say they were several sizes too small. A despairing Hamish offered me a reasonably tough pair of bush-stalking shoes, but these did not fit either. I looked at the leather Soul shoes, real 'townie' footwear, which I had worn for the drive and decided to give it a go in these. After all, the weather was fine, the tread on the shoes was really quite good, and there was no way I could disappoint my dog. In one respect at least it let me off the hook in the matter of north versus south and keeping up. 'I'll make it. I'll just be slower than you,' I announced. Thus, with city shoes, one pair of climbing socks and a pair of snow gaiters I sallied forth to do battle with the slopes.

It was quite a cool, late spring day but hot enough for me as I climbed, sweating to keep up with the tireless youths above me. Yet the shoes held up and the landmarks went by one by one: Dominie bivouac, the memorial cairn, Back Ridge hut. By nightfall we were a scant mile from Back Ridge Bivvy. My colleges undoubtedly were exasperated with my slow progress, but the other signs were good. We had seen quantities of fresh sign on the track and in the clearings en route between the two back-ridge encampments. A cold breeze had sprung up before we encountered that final well-loved hunter's favourite: an empty hut and a log book showing the last entry three weeks before. I say 'hut', but those hunters who have favoured the Back Ridge bivvy with a visit will know that this is an exaggeration, for it is of the 'dog-box' style, like a kennel with a small door to match: room only for sleeping three and not even space for a fire. Yet it was supposed to be home for the next three days, and soon developed a friendly fug as our white spirit stoves roared under the billies.

We yarned for a while, and when I ventured out at nine to drain the fluids I noticed the odd snowflake about. When I told my companions this news they considered it so curiously unseasonal as to merit a look. They dismissed it as a passing flurry, before we settled down for the night, each of us drifting off to sleep wrapped in our expectations of the next day's hunt. I woke once during the night (a common occurrence when hunting with Wredd, as she has the habit of waiting until she thinks you are asleep, then attempting to lie on top of you), and outside all was quiet. I returned to my slumberous sika hunts.

At five I was woken by Hamish's enraged attempts to open the hut door, which had mysteriously become jammed shut in the night. Only when a few well-placed boots had landed in the right place was the true cause of this discovered. It was snowed up! Eventually we managed to get the door open, emerging into a landscape transformed. A good metre of snow had fallen, and the surrounding woodland was overburdened. Soft plopping noises punctuated an otherwise deathly stillness as twig and branch slipped their loads. Still more snow arrived in great cottony flakes that clung to everything they touched.

Our situation was now, to put it simply, hazardous; mine, clad in the shoes I was, doubly so. As for my dog, how would she manage in such conditions? Vislas are not well coated and frequently shiver, even in ordinary winter temperatures. One thing was sure: we could not stay where we were. We had fuel enough only for cooking. Without a fire and with mounting drifts, a wait for rescue would be an agony of cold. We decided to head for Back Ridge hut.

Each of us put on a generous layer of clothing, topping it off with our mountain shells. Fortunately we had all had enough sense to bring snow trousers. A roll of insulating tape was pressed into service to secure the lower edge of my snow gaiters to the uppers of the shoes — a necessary precaution, otherwise soft snow would be bound to be forced into the gap as I walked, enveloping leg and foot in freezing slush. Hamish snow-raked a path from the hut to the main track, while Steve and I tidied the hut. Soon we were underway, myself the unashamed, shoe-shod, weakest of the group, trailing last along a track made easier by the passage of the others. Once we reached the main track the going became much easier, thanks to the umbrella effect of the interlocking beech tree tops. The clearings, on the other hand, were each a long battle. As we faltered along I focussed my attention on Wredd. In spite of the cold and wet she seemed to be managing famously, half-submerged in snow at times; at others vigorously shaking herself free of it. We battled on.

As we progressed upwards it became evident that on the higher ground the snow was thinner. At mid-morning we decided to try and cross back over the main range before the snow deepened and trapped us in the back-ridge area. Higher and higher we toiled, encountering then a new problem. As the open tussock faces steepened, the lead member had to climb each face twice, first falling back in a mini-avalanche of soft snow, then ascending a cleared area of slippery tussock tops.

Late in the afternoon the skies cleared and a bleary sun found us on the slopes barely thirty metres beneath the memorial cairn. Now we were battling another brand of the white menace, for on the higher slopes the wind had packed the snow hard, and this had frozen to form a thin crust. In places, the crust was strong enough to bear the weight of a person, but in others it would give way, letting the leg sink suddenly to the knee. Now each man learnt to pick his own path, going only by the shade of white to judge the best places to go. Mistakes were frequent. Only Wredd progressed effortlessly across the unbroken surface, pausing when some unfortunate was belly-deep in snow to stand adjacent and lick him encouragingly in the face.

The brightening sunlight caused a white light of such intensity as to produce that peculiar pinching pain in the eyes that signals the way to snowblindness. After a quick discussion, we burned a cardboard fragment to generate a supply of carbon that we then smeared around our eyes and cheeks to lessen reflection. Mercifully this proved enough to manage the glare and we were not driven to the next step, that of creating eyecovers with pinhole apertures.

The orange glow of evening saw us racing to complete the first downhill leg to Dominie Bivvy. From the highest ground, descent was comparatively simple. Instead of foot-sinking being a problem, it now helped anchor our legs and prevent a downward slide, as long as we did not go too fast and over-reach a knee-sink, resulting in a forward catapult face-first into the snow. We were careful, but bore in mind that speed was of the essence, for the darkening of the clearing skies would bring a frost, converting the slopes to an ice slide. Thankfully we reached Dominie Bivvy by the time the frost's full nip was in the air, and made the final torch-light descent to the carpark using rifles as hill-sticks without mishap.

Wredd leapt into the back of the 4X4 as if it were the gates of heaven and the two-litre Toyota roared into life at first kick. The noise of it and the glare of our driving lights acted as a general call to muster for three unfortunates who were stranded in the saddle hut, their car unable to make way against the half-metre of snow on the road. We headed off with a full load of trampers, packs and rifles. Slowly but surely we made it out, the snow sighing under the vehicle's belly all the way.

So ended my first trip for sika, without so much as the sight of one. In spite of this I'd had a good lesson in emergency mountaineering, plus the durability of Visla dogs and Soul shoes. Only later was I to discover that the factory that made the shoes had closed down. God knows why: they were onto a winner! **RL**

2
Equipment for alpine hunting

Alpine hunting is demanding and in order to be undertaken safely and efficiently it needs specialist equipment. In this chapter we look at climbing gear, clothing and rifles. We will emphasize the differences from gear used in normal deerstalking.

Boots and things that go on them

Most deerstalkers seem to favour light, flexible footwear, especially for bush-stalking. Many wear the common lace-up 'gummy', sometimes modified by the addition of drainer holes. The greatest advantage of such footwear is that it is quiet. In alpine hunting a quiet, sneaking approach is less crucial, and the emphasis is more on good spotting techniques. Animals are usually shot at long ranges, often in windy conditions, and so the 'luxury' of a little noise can be tolerated. So, during summer at least, most alpine hunters graduate to the more rigid (and more expensive) tramping boot.

As the lower alpine pastures are often populated with the spiky spaniard, hunters will often add canvas snow-gaiters to their usual garb of polypropylene long-johns. The canvas makes a rasping noise on vegetation, but that doesn't carry far and the canvas will effectively turn the sharp points of spaniards and the like.

For hunters who ply the mountains in the cold season, the problems multiply. A few diehards stick to their 'gummies' in winter and summer alike, but these offer poor grip in icy conditions and their open tops seem to let in a lot of snow no matter how tightly they are laced. In particular, snow is picked up when the top of the uppers sinks below the snow surface. Eventually it becomes so tightly jammed in that it begins to bruise the ankles and freeze the toes. You are forced to stop, unlace everything and clear it out. The same problem can occur to a lesser degree with other boot types. This is where snow-gaiters can again come to the rescue. They cover the top of the boot and go a good way up towards the knee, deflecting the snow.

In winter conditions, you need to decide positively whether you intend to hunt the snowfields — especially areas of frozen snow. If you decide you want to be able to roam free in the hills and go anywhere that holds game, then you need even more specialized mountaineering footwear.

When choosing boots, you can have a 'winter pair' with 'lasted' sole design, and nail along their rims special alpine hardware which sticks down below the rubber of the sole and gives grip. These tricouni nails, so useful on the snow, can, however, be a nuisance on bush trails as they catch on every twig and root. Thus you may feel you need a second pair of un-nailed ones for tramping into the hut, and also for summer use.

Or you can go for devices which you temporarily tie on your boots to give grip, for example either 'footfangs' or crampons. Before discussing these, however, a word of warning. Proper use of this type of gear is very important. If you have not been on a mountaineering course or do not have extensive alpine experience, you should not wear these on slopes steeper than 30 degrees. This means for all serious alpine hunters, such experience or instruction is mandatory.

Footfangs have a firm base which you can anchor securely to the firmer-based tramping boot. Out from the lower surface of these protrude good-sized points which give excellent grip in conditions of hard snow or ice. They are not, unfortunately, so efficient in the soft snow found at lower altitudes. This softer snow may adhere to them, building up and necessitating frequent stops to tap or kick off the encrustations. You may be better to go the whole hog and buy a set of crampons. These are thin frames of points that fit under a boot and are tied securely front and back.

Here, unfortunately, we strike yet another a problem. You can get away with wearing footfangs with a slightly flexible boot because their frame is rigid, and the only tie-point is at the back. (The front toe area of the boot hooks under a heavy overhang called a 'toe-bail'.) These two characteristics mean that the footfang actively prevents the boot from flexing. With a such a rigid setup, the boot and the footfang can't work loose and come apart. Crampons, on the other hand, are made of thin metal, often hinged in the instep, and require the more rigid mountaineering-type boot.

Equipment for alpine hunting

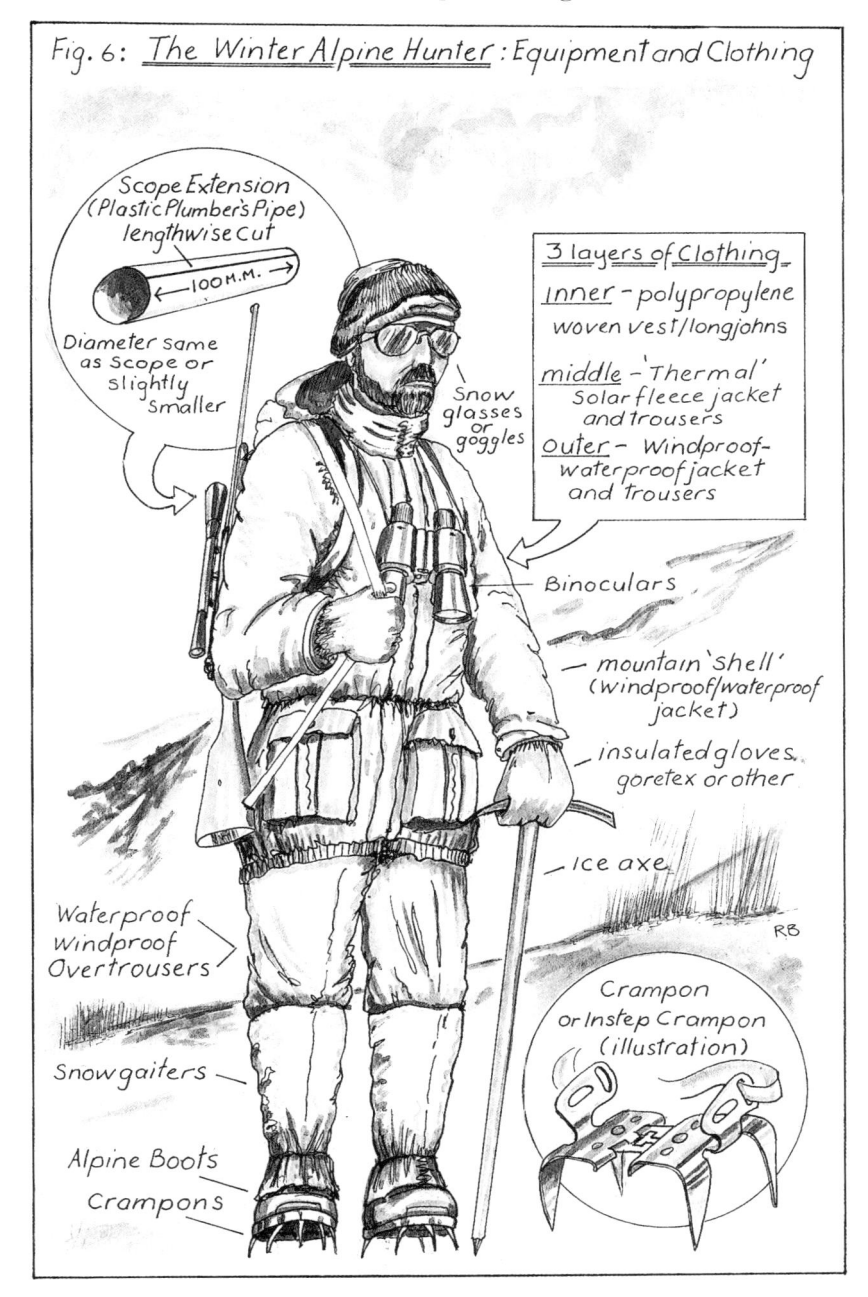

Fig. 6: The Winter Alpine Hunter: Equipment and Clothing

Scope Extension (Plastic Plumber's Pipe) lengthwise cut — 100 M.M. — Diameter same as scope or slightly smaller

3 layers of Clothing
- **Inner** — polypropylene woven vest/longjohns
- **middle** — 'Thermal' Solar fleece jacket and trousers
- **Outer** — Windproof-waterproof jacket and trousers

Snow glasses or goggles

Binoculars

mountain 'shell' (windproof/waterproof jacket)

insulated gloves, goretex or other

Ice axe

Waterproof Windproof Overtrousers

Snow gaiters

Alpine Boots
Crampons

Crampon or Instep Crampon (illustration)

The best way to buy mountaineering boots is to go into a reputable mountaineering shop and either take your crampons with you or, better still, buy both boots and crampons at the same time. To gauge a proper fit, the frame of the crampon should fit the boot on all sides and remain attached when the boot is lifted off the ground with the crampon straps undone.

Don't buy crampons that have straight, forward-facing points at the front: these are for specialist ice-work. And don't carry them inside your pack as they are liable to puncture your plastic food containers. Tie them on top of your pack, and be careful how you take your pack on and off to avoid spiking anybody. To avoid stepping on the spikes in bare feet, take care where you store them in and around camp.

Yet another possible solution is to use instep crampons. These are small platforms of spikes designed to strap onto the instep of your boots. They are light and portable and can be used with flexible tramping boots. Their main disadvantage is that they provide no grip for the toe and heel areas of the boot — the very areas most people instinctively use as weight-bearing points. Thus when wearing them you have to clump about, deliberately placing the whole sole down in a single action. Because instep crampons do not fit precisely around the edge of the boot, much greater strain is placed on the bindings. If you do buy these devices, make sure you get proper bindings for them and keep them tight.

Ice axes

Ice axes are the basic tool of mountaineering. They were invented and in widespread use before crampons, and to some extent are a substitute for them — you can almost always cut a series of steps across a steep frozen face and cross it without wearing crampons. But that is much harder work and most mountaineers would insist that both ice axes and crampons be used together.

The head of the ice axe is used for cutting steps in snow and ice, while the other end has a metal point which gives grip when you are using the axe as a walking stick. There are other uses too, such as in the important procedure of 'self-arrest'. This is a technique whereby the ice axe is used to stop a fall down a mountainside. (We don't go into these other techniques here, but remind you again of the importance of proper instruction.)

There are many designs of ice-axe head and various lengths of shaft. Speaking generally, the hunter needs an axe with a gently curved head (don't go for the ones with steeply sloping faces that have a 'pterodactyl-like' appearance — these are designed for specialist ice work). Longer-shafted axes make better walking sticks on the flat and on gentle slopes. Unlike mountaineers, hunters spend most of their time on slopes below 45 degrees. A axe with a overall length of about 70 cm will be long enough for handy use in the walking-stick mode. A non-metal shaft will enable you to hold it in cold conditions while wearing only light gloves.

If you are going to use an ice axe, then you must have a rifle sling and know your sling techniques (see p.40), or you will find that you run out of hands!

Before buying any of this specialized gear, get the advice of an expert mountaineer — not only advice on what to buy, but how to learn to use it. Go out with them in the snow and learn how to use the gear on the job. Wrongly used, mountaineering gear can be more of a danger than a help.

Clothing

Some hunters are fond enough of their beloved 'swannies' to wear them on the higher slopes. Even in summer, however, they soon discover that the excellent non-rustle material provides little barrier to a cold wind. Windproof gear (including leggings) can make the world of difference in summer, and are essential in winter. Although windproofs rasp badly against vegetation, they can save the flesh from literally freezing onto the fibre of your long-johns. Windproof gear is usually also made to be waterproof.

You can go for the old-fashioned materials that stop wind and any moisture (which also means locking up sweat on their inner surface), or you can go for the more expensive, breathable fabrics such as Gore-Tex, Entrant or Milair. These will keep out wind and rain as well as vent the sweat and condensation. However, a word of caution: the actual material is usually quite thin and easily torn, especially when bush-bashing. To counter this, heavyweight fabrics are used in the construction of durable mountain jackets. These still have the same breathable fabric inside, but over this is a layer of tougher protective material. Not many jackets made of these synthetic materials use natural colours such green, white or light grey. Usually they are only sold in safety-type day-glo colours. These garish colours rather go against the grain of New Zealand hunters, who like to blend into the landscape rather than stand out. Then again, perhaps it is a good thing in terms of shooting safety, for our game animals are to a large extent colour-blind. It is probably only we humans who are dazzled by the bright colours.

Once a hunter becomes accustomed to wearing jackets made from synthetic windproof materials, the next step is synthetic 'polar-fleece'-type undergarments. These are light, cram down well in the pack, and are easier to dry out than woollens, yet they also stay warm when wet. The only drawback we have discovered is their tendency to smell a bit when loaded with a few days' sweat, but new versions are on the way that counter even this problem.

Two weights of garment are available; a single layer with fluff on one side only for summer wear and a winter weight with fluff inside and out. Under these garments we recommend and use an innermost layer consisting of a plain polypropylene vest and long-johns. Again, these are available in summer and winter weights, but we recommend the heavier winter weight long-johns for all seasons as they are much more snag-resistant.

On icy days in winter when the southerlies blow, even all this will occasionally not be enough. Then a down jacket (real down or a synthetic fibre) can be added or substituted for the polar-fleece layer. These jackets are extremely light and can not only be crammed right down into a small carry sack, but also be used as a luxurious pillow at night.

Choosing socks for alpine hunting is more difficult. Synthetic fibre socks (e.g., polypropylene) are light and do not suck up water from melting snow, but they are much harder on the feet than natural fibre. Hunters walking long distances in pure synthetic socks are liable to find their feet worn raw. It may thus be advisable to settle for the more old-fashioned but less abrasive fibres. Some hunters compromise by wearing socks made with a mixture of natural and synthetic yarns.

Gloves are essential in winter, when the naked flesh of your hand can attach itself in a painful manner to the metal parts of your rifle. Gloves, however, make it more difficult to use a rifle. A workable solution is to use two pairs: thin, knitted polypropylene gloves when hunting and, for in-between times, either a thicker, quilted fibre-filled pair or greasy wool mittens that fit over the polypropylene ones.

Snowblindness and sunburn

Even in cloudy conditions the ultra-violet comes straight through and you must protect your eyes and skin. Proper snow goggles are best, as these protect from the side as well as through the lenses. Good sunglasses, e.g., Polaroids, will do at a pinch. Snowblindness is a terrible affliction and the effects do not begin to be felt until it is too late to cover up. It feels like sand under the eyelids.

Protect your skin, too, from the extra ultra-violet of snowy, high-altitude conditions. Zinc ointment is best, but good sun cream will do. Apply to all exposed skin, including ears, under the nose and chin, and inside nostrils. Lips are sensitive to wind as well as sun — there is nothing quite like badly chapped lips to spoil the pleasure of your trip, so an ultraviolet-proof salve stick is a good investment.

Headgear

You will usually need something to wear on your head to protect against heat loss and, in some situations, falling rocks and stones.

A balaclava is a good idea to cut down heat loss, and it is less likely to be blown off than a hat. One with a built-in peak will protect you from the sun, rain and falling snow. Most windproof mountain jackets come with a peaked hood, to be pulled up and over your ears and head. Most hunters, however, prefer not to wear them as they restrict vision and hearing.

A hunter wishing to live a long life avoids steep and bluffy places when avalanches are possible. These spots are much safer when conditions are stable and firm, but even then there can still be problems with frost heave. A climber's helmet can give you some protection, especially when worn at the base of bluffs when the sun first hits after a frosty night. Helmets also give protection from falling rocks dislodged from above by your mate when you are following behind up a steep place.

Rifle and sling

Rifle slings are often of no consequence to down-country hunters, some of whom don't ever use them. High up on the alpine slopes, however, a proper sling correctly used is vital for safety.

When navigating difficult country, and especially when carrying an ice axe ready for use, your rifle needs to be slung securely from your shoulder. It should not, however, be slung diagonally across your back. In this position it is more likely to be damaged if you slip or fall. More importantly, it cannot be readily unslung.

Apart from when game is sighted, speedy unslinging is needed in two other situations. Firstly, as we have seen, if you are caught in an avalanche or in an area that is about to avalanche. Secondly, if you slip on a smooth surface when you are not carrying an ice axe, you can unsling the weapon and use it in a rifle-assisted self arrest.

To do this, you unsling the rifle, grasp the small of the butt (the pistol grip) firmly with one hand and the fore end of the butt tightly with the other. Gripping the rifle this way, hold it diagonally across your front. Then roll onto your front and at the same time angle the weapon so that the thick end of the butt points outwards, faces downwards and digs in. As the butt digs in, the rifle will be pulled upwards. You need to tense your arms to maintain a position where the butt is projecting out just in front of your lower chest with your weight bearing on it. (Note: attempting to dig the barrel-end in usually results in a gun with a bent barrel and an alarmed hunter both being catapulted in opposite directions. (Roger has tried sticking the barrel in and got this result. He has only tried it once!)

When climbing up or down, it is common to walk on a diagonal line across the slope. Therefore, either your right or your left side faces the slope. Your rifle should be mounted on the shoulder that is furthermost away from the slope. The reason for this is simply that, should you slip, you will not fall upon the telescopic sight and knock it so it shoots off the point of aim, or even damage it or the rifle in the fall. On zig-zag ascents and descents, this means a momentary halt to change the rifle from one shoulder to the other at the end of each traverse. This can be a little tiresome, but with sufficient practice it will become second nature.

The sling itself should be narrow (no greater than 30 mm) so that it digs into the clothing on your shoulder and thus gives a better grip. Some alpine hunters even boost the grip of the front third of the sling that lies over the shoulder proper by attaching a piece of velcro hook material to its inner surface. In contrast, lowland hunters often favour a sling that is wide where it touches the shoulder, so it does not dig in uncomfortably. However, a wide sling is more likely to slip off than a narrow one, especially when worn over slippery waterproof or windproof gear. When alpine hunting, you will usually be wearing two or more layers of clothing, so a narrow sling seldom feels uncomfortable.

The points of attachment of the sling to the rifle need to be strong. In ex-factory rifles it is common for the fore-end sling attachment to be held onto the stock by a simple short wood screw. On becoming saturated, this attachment typically weakens, and one day lets go with no warning. It is better to have an attachment using only metal gripping onto metal. A metal bolt screwed into a metal plate recessed into the inside of the fore end is more secure. The sling attachment at the butt end of the stock can be held there by a long wood screw going very deep into the thick wood of the butt.

Synthetic stocks are increasingly being used as they have the advantage of resistance to swelling when damp and are often lighter. Nevertheless, there are disadvantages with synthetic stocks, depending on the type — many different materials are used.

Earlier types of stock, made by injection moulding and without internal reinforcing, are liable to distort when left in the sun. A particular trap for the unwary is to leave them in the sun on the back shelf of a locked and parked vehicle (a practice which is now in any case illegal.) They can also split in very cold conditions — especially if put under a strain, as when being used for self-arrest.

Nowadays another type, the 'hollow-fill', stock is more common. It usually consists of a central core of light foamy plastic covered with a tougher skin of plastic or fibreglass. Hollow-fill stocks can be distinguished from solid ones by their lightness and the hollow sound they make when tapped. (This 'drumming' quality is one which many bush-stalkers view as a noise-making disadvantage.)

Hollow-fill stocks with a plastic skin share the same problem as moulded stocks in extremes of temperature. Also, under heavy use the thin plastic coat may not be strong and durable enough to cope with the wear and strain of the sling. To deal with this problem, some manufacturers incorporate solid blocks of reinforcing material at the two sling attachment points. Generally, they are not tough enough to stand the occasional heavy bash against rocks that rifles inevitably get when alpine hunting.

With fibreglass-skinned hollow-fill stocks there is less of a problem with temperature extremes and accidental bashes on rocks, but the sling-attachment problem remains. You would do well to check whether it is possible to obtain the rifle in a range of skin thicknesses and go for the thickest you can get.

With any synthetic stock you should check that the toe of the butt (the bottom of the end that goes against your shoulder when firing) is reinforced, to give the required strength in self-arrest procedures.

Despite these problems, a number of high-quality stocks well suited to alpine work are starting to appear. The best ones usually have internal reinforcing of carbon fibre or kevlar threads. When buying hunting equipment you tend to get what you pay for. But don't blindly assume that expense equals quality. It is worth giving this whole, rather complex, subject a bit of research before any purchase is made.

Any rifle stock should be strong enough to withstand use as a self-arrest aid. Wooden stocks should have a tough, well-mounted metal butt plate. Many types of rifle actions are available, but most alpine hunters favour bolt actions. These are less liable to freeze up, and, if they do, are more easily forced open. If possible, buy a model with a flash-hider on the end. This can help prevent the barrel clogging with snow during a fall, although even then it is a good idea to carry a coiled steel-wire cleaning rod.

All 'scopes should be fitted with some system to prevent snow from packing into the ends. A 'scope end covered in frozen snow is much more difficult to clear quickly than one that is simply wet or muddy. Various alternatives can be considered, for example a set of quick-detach 'scope covers or a piece of rubber inner tube cut like a giant rubber band.

Lastly, for those hunters who like to be ready for instant action and cannot bear to have lenses covered, consider making a front-end 'scope extension piece from a segment of plastic plumbing pipe (see fig.6). This attachment will not only act as a barrier to snow, but also prevent snow glare from reflecting off the upper rim of the forward lens and into the 'scope.

'Scopes need to be robust and securely mounted, preferably with the modern continental rail-mount, which is less likely to catch on bulky alpine clothing or to accumulate snow. It is a good idea to rubber-tape the 'scope tube and rifle barrel to help prevent the metal from freezing to your skin in cold conditions.

Because of the greater ranges at which alpine game is shot, a 'scope of higher magnification is usually chosen, sometimes up to 15 power — although at this extreme magnification it will usually be a vari-power model with other lower-power settings. A 'scope of this impressive magnification is able to double to some extent as a spotting 'scope.

Finally, we come to the choice of rifle calibre (see also Appendix

Equipment for alpine hunting

2). Because of greater ranges (commonly up to 300 metres) a flatter-shooting calibre is required. Here, however, chamois and tahr hunters part company, at least in theory. Chamois are lighter beasts than deer and are thin-skinned. They are easily downed by smaller calibres such as the .243. On the other hand, tahr are large animals, often equal in weight to a full-grown red stag. They also have a hide that can be over 25 mm thick at their chest. This is a much tougher barrier to a bullet than the hide of a red stag. So for tahr, a heavier projectile with 'harder' expansion characteristics is needed for better penetration of the hide. Often you need to drop the animal quickly and cleanly before it hurls itself from the place you saw it to some other inaccessible spot. Such good tahr rifle characteristics are better found in calibres such as the 7 mm Remington magnum or the other magnums.

What then is the hunter who wants to shoot both tahr and chamois to do? We offer two suggestions. You can choose a rifle that has good tahr characteristics, and put up with overkill on chamois. Or you can handload two different loads with different projectiles, for the same rifle. Often this results in differing points of impact of the two loads, and this needs to be allowed for at any given range, but it is not as difficult as it sounds. Roger had at one time a 7 mm Remington magnum in which he used factory Remington core-locked 150-grain loads for tahr and for chamois a handload that was taken from the recipe for a 7 x 57 but loaded in the 7 mm Remington magnum cases behind a 115-grain Speer hollow-point bullet. The two loads shot very close together at 180 metres.

When using two loads that have similar projectiles, it is a good idea to put a little ring of coloured indelible felt-tip marker around the edge of the primer in case the two lots get mixed up.

Binoculars

Binoculars are essential and, generally speaking, the bigger the better. Go for good-quality lenses with moderate magnification but big apertures to give excellent clarity at distance. Waterproof models, with their all-weather characteristic, are best. The modern autofocus type is particularly good because there is no rotating focus-wheel assemblage to let in the damp. They can, however, be difficult to use in conditions of low light intensity, as they tend to produce ghost images.

On just about every set of binoculars you will find a set of numbers that reads something like 7 x 55, or 12 x 20. The first figure is the magnification, like the magnification figure that you have on your scope. Thus if you own a 2-to-7-power 'scope and buy 7 x 55 binoculars you will end up with two devices capable of the same magnification.

The second figure is the diameter in millimetres of the front lens. It is important because it tells you how much light is entering the front of the binoculars. The more light coming in the front, the brighter the image that reaches your eye, as it is concentrated before coming out of the (smaller) back eyepiece lens. Thus in low light conditions you will see better through binoculars with a bigger front lens. The scene will also be sharper and more detailed. Even a small increase in front-lens size produces a large increase in the amount of light it collects and so can make a significant difference. (For example, from 7 x 30 to 7 x 35 is only a 5 mm difference in lens size but it lets in a third more light.)

To explain binocular specifications more clearly, consider two very different outfits: 7 x 55's and 10 x 20's. The 7 x 55 pair has a front lens measuring 35 mm more in diameter than a 10 x 20 pair, and so would undoubtedly be better in low light conditions, and give a clearer picture in all conditions. Although the 10 x 20's have a greater magnification, they will probably be less effective for spotting animals at distance on a mountainside for two reasons. Firstly, they do not give such as sharp a picture. Secondly, owing to the higher magnification they have a smaller field of vision. A hunter uses binoculars specifically to scan large areas of ground, looking for animals made small by distance. If you already know where the animals are, you can use your 'scope to view them, and not bother with binoculars.

Using binoculars with too high a magnification is a bit like searching the inside of a dark barn with a powerful penlight-type torch. You see only a tiny bit of ground at a time. Using the 7 x 55 binoculars, on the other hand, is like searching with an ordinary wide-beam torch. The 'picture' may not be so sharp, but the operation is still more efficient, covering more ground at a time and is thus better suited to the hunter's purpose.

On the face of it then you would do best to purchase the biggest-lensed pair you can buy with moderate magnification, say 8 x 150's! But there are disadvantages here too. The bigger the lenses the more heavy and bulky the binoculars. You would soon swap your 8 x 150's for a lighter pair such as 8 x 30's or 7 x 35's, which are popular for deerstalking because they are light and compact. And there is the cost factor: bigger binoculars cost a lot more. However, for alpine hunting, binoculars are so crucial to success that the cost and the extra effort of carrying a larger pair may be justified. It may be a good idea to try a variety of your mates' pairs before you make a final choice. (A friend of Roger's swears by 8 x 50's. As a compensation for their bulk, he also uses them as a portable and accurate rifle rest by opening them out and lying them on the ground. The fore-end of his rifle fits quite snugly between the rubber-coated tubes of the binoculars.)

Some alpine hunters carry spotting 'scopes as well as binoculars. They use these to minutely examine likely areas at long range, and also for judging animals for trophy potential. This benefit can be also achieved, to some extent, by the use of a vari-power rifle 'scope with a large aperture and high upper magnification. This use, secondary to binoculars, is particularly favoured by tahr hunters.

Variable-power zoom-lens binoculars are starting to become available, but they do not have much to offer the alpine hunter, particularly if you are using a spotting 'scope or a high magnification vari-power rifle-scope.

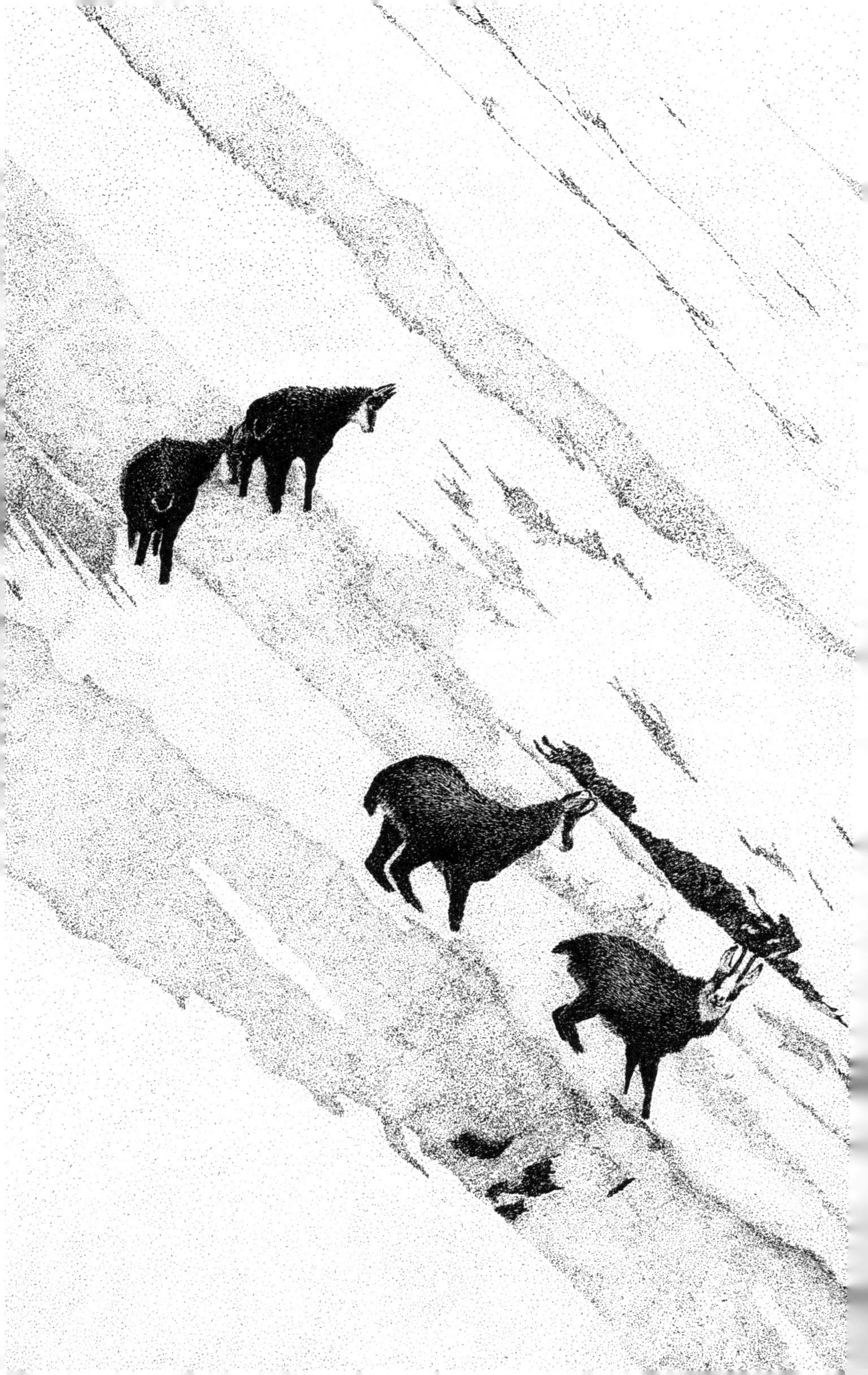

Chamois

*Do you know of the long day's patience,
belly down on frozen drift,
While the head of heads is feeding
out of range?*

Rudyard Kipling

3
Hunting chamois

We climbed, my farmer friend and I, up through snow tussocks coloured the rich yellow-brown of late summer. The rising sun still lingered at the dark rock rim of the opposite side of the valley, illuminating the high peaks above us with growing strength. The misty path of its rays was visible as they streamed over the valley's edge, promising another scorching day. Up through the alpine meadows we climbed and climbed, until our lungs were heaving, eager to complete the ascent while the air was cool. We continued upward until, by the time the touch of heat at our backs signalled the sun was well up, we emerged breathless at the fellfield's upper edge.

'Time for a spell and a look,' said Garth. We crunched across a minor scree to a protruding rock stack, leaning across its top to glass the country about and below us. There was a long pause, each of us intent on spotting, privately drinking in the morning's beauty. Nothing. We examined every rockstack's shadowed foot, probed every tussock-clad basin. Still nothing.

The light up-slope of the catabatic was well established by the time we rose and started the main business of the day, a long traverse up-valley above the fellfields yet well below the ridgeline's grey rock peaks. We crossed basin after basin, pausing as we breasted each successive side-ridge to glass the slopes freshly revealed. Glassing became more difficult as the day's heat gripped rock and scree, producing a shimmering mirage. By mid-day we had progressed five kilometres and disturbed only a native falcon, its mournful, piercing cry audible for miles as it diminished to a distant speck before vanishing below.

We chose a ridge crest that offered some shelter from the sun and settled to munch biersticks with our fruit juice. We both succumbed to the early start and hard morning's work and dozed off.

By the time we woke (to the attentions of a wasp, no less! God knows what it hoped to find at such heights), the sun had started its decline. We gathered our day-packs and glassed again before commencing our reluctant return, the wind now resolute at our backs. To try new ground we dipped lower, even though it meant frequent ups and downs to negotiate a number of rocky bluffs.

We were about to pick our way across the top of one of the bluffs when my mate dislodged a rock. It skittered noisily down the bluff face. Then came a sharp whistle. We looked down, craning our necks to scan the fifteen metres to the base of the bluffs. Another whistle. Then, off to the left a shower of gravel cascaded down between two rock pillars. We had found them.

Still we couldn't spot them — but this also meant they (or it) couldn't spot us. We elected to play a waiting game, withdrawing from the bluff edge to sit quietly, suppressing our mounting excitement. We heard no further rockfalls or whistles. Traversing stealthily back up-valley we reached a place where a steep ridge clad in stunted tussock dropped down on the up-valley side of the little bluff. We crept down, fearful of dislodging the fine gravel that was visible between the greenery. A scant ten-metre descent and the ridgeline ended abruptly. We inched to the edge and peered over.

Below us was a ten-metre rockface and below that a well-rounded, tussock-clad shoulder. On this shoulder were two chamois, quietly grazing, totally unaware of our presence. I admired their rosy-brown summer coats. In whispered conversation we arrived at the conclusion that they were does. Garth tried to get his camera out of his daypack but in doing so dislodged another stone. Down it went with the usual crash and the chamois were alerted. They ran down the shoulder, the larger animal in the lead. They stopped. Then, incredibly, they turned and ran back up again. At the very base of the rockface they halted again. The larger animal stamped and whistled.

At this point I was leaning well out over the rim of the bluff in order to get a view, and in doing so caused a large slab of rock to detach itself. I felt myself going, and clawed to maintain my grip, legs flailing. I got the situation in hand just in time to hear the slab crash-landing on the slopes below. The animals were nowhere to be seen and my mate wore an exasperated expression.

We started to retrace our steps up the treacherous ridgeline. Suddenly Garth gave a start and pointed off to a ridge upvalley about 150 metres away. On this ridge, about thirty metres above us, a large chamois buck was standing looking directly at us. He must have heard all the noise and come down to see what was happening. Two rifles roared and we heard the thud of bullet strike.

I let Garth do the retrieval. He's a high-country farmer after all, and fitter than me, I told myself. I sat and looked down the mountain, out onto the Canterbury Plains with their blue-grey coat of late afternoon haze. From way below, the faint sound of a sheep truck labouring up the Tekapo incline told me of another world, of work and obligations. 'Wait for me,' I called, and hurried to help my farmer friend and savour the alpine hunting experience to the last. **RL**

From their release point at Mt Cook in 1907, chamois dispersed quickly and now occupy a large area of the Southern Alps. They have spread to other South Island ranges too. Chamois behaviour has been much studied both here and in the European alps, their native home.

The scientific name for chamois, *Rupicapra rupicapra*, literally means rock goat, as 'rupi' is rock and 'capra' is goat in Latin. This name highlights the common ancestry of goats and chamois. You have probably hunted deer, and who hasn't shot a few feral goats at some time in their career as a hunter? Chamois are more like goats than deer, so if you haven't hunted chamois before use more of your goat-hunting experience as a guide, and less of your deer-hunting instincts.

Comparing chamois and goats we find two important similarities. Firstly, when evening comes, goats simply sit down for the night and are to be found in the same spot at daybreak. Unlike deer, they don't eat at night. The same is true of chamois. Chamois wander by day and rest by night. However, there is one exception to this rule. Recent studies show some New Zealand chamois undertake their spring and autumn migrations at night when the snow is hardened by frost (see p. 53).

Secondly, goats can eat most species of plant. They also eat many of the different parts of a plant: leaves, small twigs, bark, flowers and so on. Chamois are rather like this as well. In 1961, a German scientist, Fuschlberger, summarized the behaviour of Northern hemisphere chamois by saying, 'It eats just about everything that is green.' This largely holds true in New Zealand too, although they do eat berries as well, and shun a few plant species.

When hunting deer, knowing the plant species they are feeding on is very helpful to the hunter. But with chamois, such knowledge is less useful, because the animals eat mainly grasses and herbs which are smaller and more difficult to identify. For chamois, a good understanding of their movement patterns and herd migration traditions is more useful. We discuss these below.

Tolerance of extreme cold is another characteristic of chamois, but not one they share with goats. It is a common belief among scientists that chamois specifically evolved during one of the past ice ages to exploit the cold alpine environments of the ancient European mountains. To do so, they developed the ability to freely walk on ice and snow and keep warm in freezing weather. These qualities, together with the ability to thrive on a broader range of plant species, enabled the animals to live at higher elevations than deer. So successful is this adaptation that at times New Zealand chamois actually find their environment too hot! As a consequence, they have developed some peculiar behaviour for cooling off, especially when they are wearing their winter coat (see p. 60).

Range and territory

Because chamois live in a more open environment than deer they are easier to study and much has been learned about them and their behaviour in New Zealand. The way they establish their territories and move about within them enables the chamois to exploit most of the grazing reserves available within their southern mountain range.

We will first consider the movement patterns of chamois point by point.

The big picture: two types of population
From the time of release in 1907 until the early 1970s, chamois extended their range and their numbers increased. However, since the 1970s they have not significantly increased their range, and their herd and migration patterns have probably stabilized and become more predictable.

Keen chamois hunters over the years have built up a detailed knowledge of animal behaviour in their favoured hunting grounds. From the 1970s onwards, chamois hunters began reporting two distinct types of hunting area: those offering good hunting year-round (although perhaps with more animals present in the warmer months), and those areas which only held animals during particular seasons. As far as the seasonally good hunting places were concerned, good winter-hunting places were more common in the headwaters of the West Coast rivers, whereas the good summer hunting places were more common in headwaters east of the main divide. It seemed almost as though there were two distinct sub-species of chamois,

Fig. 7: Migratory Movements of the Chamois of the Southern Alps

WESTERN SLOPES
Winter warmer and wetter

EASTERN SLOPES
Summer warmer

Traditional migration routes?

Wintering

Spring Summer early autumn

Floater Populations

Input when vacancies occur (mature animals)

Output when overpopulated (juveniles)

Permanent Populations

and indeed this was fervently believed by some very experienced and knowledgeable shooters.

It took a research programme using snare collars for tagging individual animals to find out the truth, by tracking movements of tagged chamois throughout the year. This and other studies suggest that our New Zealand chamois have evolved herd dynamics that are unique to this country.

In the year-round hunting areas, a number of individuals live in a group and are able to be permanent residents of their area because there is an adequate food supply at all seasons. Most importantly, there is food in winter. It is this that probably limits the number of animals that can be permanently resident in the area.

In the seasonal hunting areas, forage is only available for a short time on a seasonal basis. The summer seasonal areas are normally found east of the main divide, often adjacent to the year-round permanent residence areas. The winter seasonal areas are generally in places with warmer winter weather, mostly west of the main divide where milder winters promote a longer growing season for food plants.

By identifying tagged animals, it has been shown that the animals on winter seasonal grounds are the same ones that are to be found in summer on the summer seasonal grounds. This shows clearly that the animals migrate each year between seasonal pastures. An inner impulse (probably triggered by a shortage of food, or perhaps minerals) causes them to quit their winter grounds of typically shadowy peaks on the western side of the ranges in early spring and head for the more sunny eastern slopes. Biologists call these animals 'floaters'.

To make such journeys means making high alpine crossings, and you would expect them to wait for the worst of the winter snow to melt before setting off. However, observations show this is not the case: the chamois leave before the snows melt. The bucks tend to depart first; then, when the snows are a little thinner, the does and kids follow. It seems that weather providing clear spring days and frosty nights is favoured, and that the migrants often travel at night. A frosty night produces a firm crust on top of the snow, which the animals obviously find easier going than deep soft snow.

A few days of clear weather in early spring, therefore, may result in an influx of animals onto the spring seasonal hunting grounds east of the Southern Alps that have hitherto been rather deserted.

One fascinating thing about chamois migration routes is that they don't always use the easy routes we humans would instinctively take, such as the high alpine passes. Their traditional routes often cross bluffs and rock faces — perhaps chosen to avoid black ice, soft snow or possibly to give access to food en route. (See Fig. 7.)

Another important observation from tagged chamois is the striking replenishment of groups occupying the year-round chamois areas where numbers have been reduced by intensive hunting. Migrating 'floater' animals that venture into the territories of permanent populations may be 'adopted', abandon their migratory life and thus become part of that resident population. The animals most likely to make this simple change are does, while the behaviour of bucks is somewhat more complex (see p. 57–59).

In summary, the overall chamois population shows two types of behaviour. There are small resident groups in good year-round food-producing areas, and floaters, which migrate between one seasonal food supply and another. However, some floaters may become permanent residents if they enter an area with a year-round food supply that has a vacancy for them. Generally speaking, the proportion of males is higher in the floater population.

Hunting tips from population movement studies

Try to work out whether your hunting grounds contain permanent residents or floater populations. This should enable you to divide your various hunting country into year-round, spring, summer and winter-only areas. Such a classification will enable you to concentrate on the places most likely to hold animals at the time of year you are hunting.

It will also enable you to improve your chances of encountering a buck, by targeting the floater population. However, you should note that a mature buck living within a permanent group on good tucker has a better opportunity to grow a trophy head. On the other hand, hunting grounds with permanent populations often become well known and so attract a lot of hunter attention, which may not be the case with the more dispersed and intermittent seasonal grazing areas.

By working out the seasonal movements of a particular herd of floaters you may be able to plan a stalk to intercept them on their migration routes while they are crossing high barren terrain where they are easier to spot. For some areas in the Southern Alps these migrations have been worked out in detail (see Fig. 8). Elsewhere, careful observation and recording of chamois tracks, particularly on spring and autumn snows, may enable you to build up your own

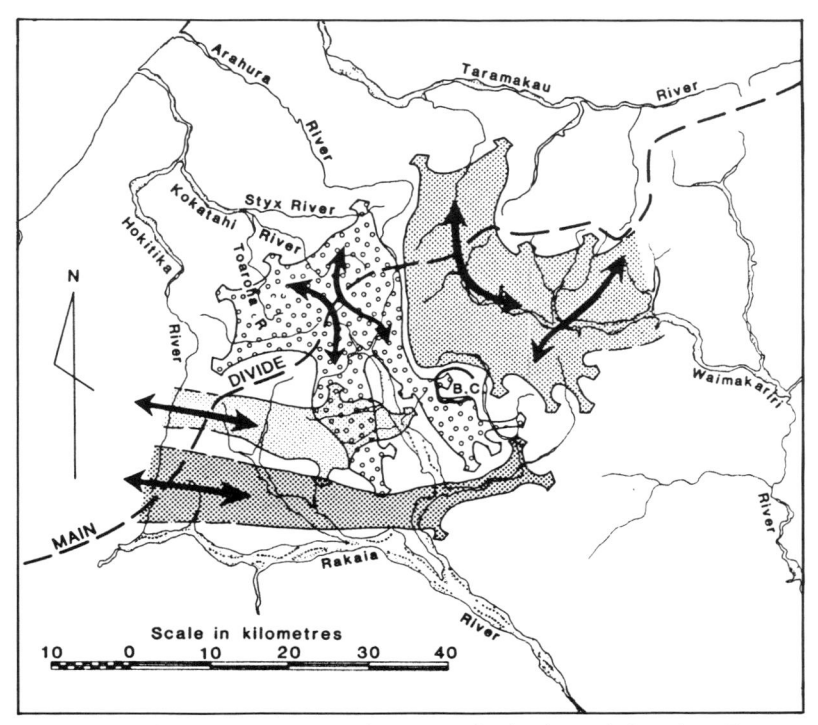

Fig. 8: Major chamois migration routes between Westland and central Canterbury. From C.M.H. Clarke in the New Zealand Journal of Zoology *(1986).*

knowledge and prediction scheme for tracking the migrations. Even if you don't actually catch them while they are migrating, you at least stand a good chance of being the first hunter on the spot when they reach their new seasonal area. A day-by-day diary recording local weather and sightings of animals or their tracks is prime data for predicting future movements. This is particularly relevant in early spring, when clear frosty weather is likely to trigger migrations.

A final implication of the interaction of the floater and resident groups is one of chamois management. From time to time chamois are subject to disease. Where a floater population exists around a diseased resident one, you can engage in some first-line management of the resident group by vigorously culling out those beasts that are diseased. Their places are likely to be taken up by individuals from the floater population that (hopefully) are healthy animals.

The local scene: day-to-day details

So far we have considered the major seasonal movements of chamois. Now we will look at what influences their day-by-day movements to build up a local picture of the typical day in the life of a chamois, whether it belongs to the permanent or floater population. Food type and rutting behaviour are discussed later.

Herd size

Food availability determines the size of permanent chamois herds. Similarly, the amount of food available in any temporary area during the time it is being utilized by a floater population will determine how many animals graze there and for how long.

Compared to European alpine pastures, the alpine pastures in New Zealand are relatively poor in animal forage. As a consequence, chamois herd size here in New Zealand is smaller. Groups of up to 16 chamois have been recorded in New Zealand, but compare this with a herd of 208 individuals recorded from France in the western Pyrenees. The poorer pastures here mean the chamois have to spread out more, and move about more, in order to get a reasonable daily intake. Thus, grazing chamois in New Zealand normally are thinly scattered across the landscape and relatively mobile even in good grazing areas. Most chamois are therefore encountered singly or in groups of two or occasionally three animals. Overall, however, this leads to a higher chance of an encounter between hunter and chamois than if all the animals were concentrated in one large herd.

Social habit

Another factor leading to wide dispersal of herds is the relatively weak social force binding the individuals together in any one group. Even in the predominantly female permanent resident populations there is little social force binding the group together — a situation quite different to that in red deer hind groups, for example. However, in female chamois society some structure does exist. This is a sort of 'pecking order' where the dominant doe takes the best feeding and shelter spots and warns other lesser beasts away by a series of meaningful body postures. But bonding between members of the larger group is weak.

As we have seen, resident groups in New Zealand seem content to allow floater populations to wander into their area. This is evidence that the occupying animals are not particularly concerned with defending their area against outsiders. In contrast, in the more densely populated areas of Europe, female chamois have been seen fighting and even goring trespassing does. Perhaps in Europe there are areas of high-quality alpine pasture worth fighting over while in New Zealand there are no exceptional areas worthy of the effort needed to defend them. It may be that our chamois reserve their energy for wandering and searching for food.

All this shows that in New Zealand the basic chamois social unit is one chamois on its own, or the situation of the doe and her kid. Aggregation of these basic units into larger groups is largely a matter of chance, for example when a number of chamois all head for the same shelter in a storm. Once the storm is over, they are liable to separate and only re-combine in different chance groups of strangers at another time as a result of another similar event. Therefore, if a trophy buck is seen in a group one day you cannot count on it being in the same group the next day. In fact you cannot even count on the group still being in existence. Chances are the buck will be on its own somewhere else the next day, continuing its own individual wanderings.

Sexual differences

As with red deer, there is in chamois society an all-pervading behavioural difference between the two sexes that persists through the year.

As we have seen, the does, usually with a kid close by, tend to associate loosely with other does. The bucks, for their part, are usually found in separate areas, and in New Zealand at least seem to prefer a solitary existence. This is not to say that numbers of males will never be found living alongside each other in certain areas. However, when grazing, bucks will be well separated and encountered singly. It seems to be a good general rule that if you see two animals grazing close to one another in any season other than the rut the larger one will be a doe and the smaller a yearling.

This tendency for bucks to be solitary is not, however, universal. In the densely populated areas of the Pyrenees, larger more cohesive groups of female chamois form and bucks band together in separate bachelor groups. This has not been recorded in New Zealand, but conceivably could occur in areas of fertile pasture and denser populations.

From February through to March a complex series of animal movements involving male and migrant female populations begin. These movements affect group size as well as population densities

Alpine Hunting in New Zealand

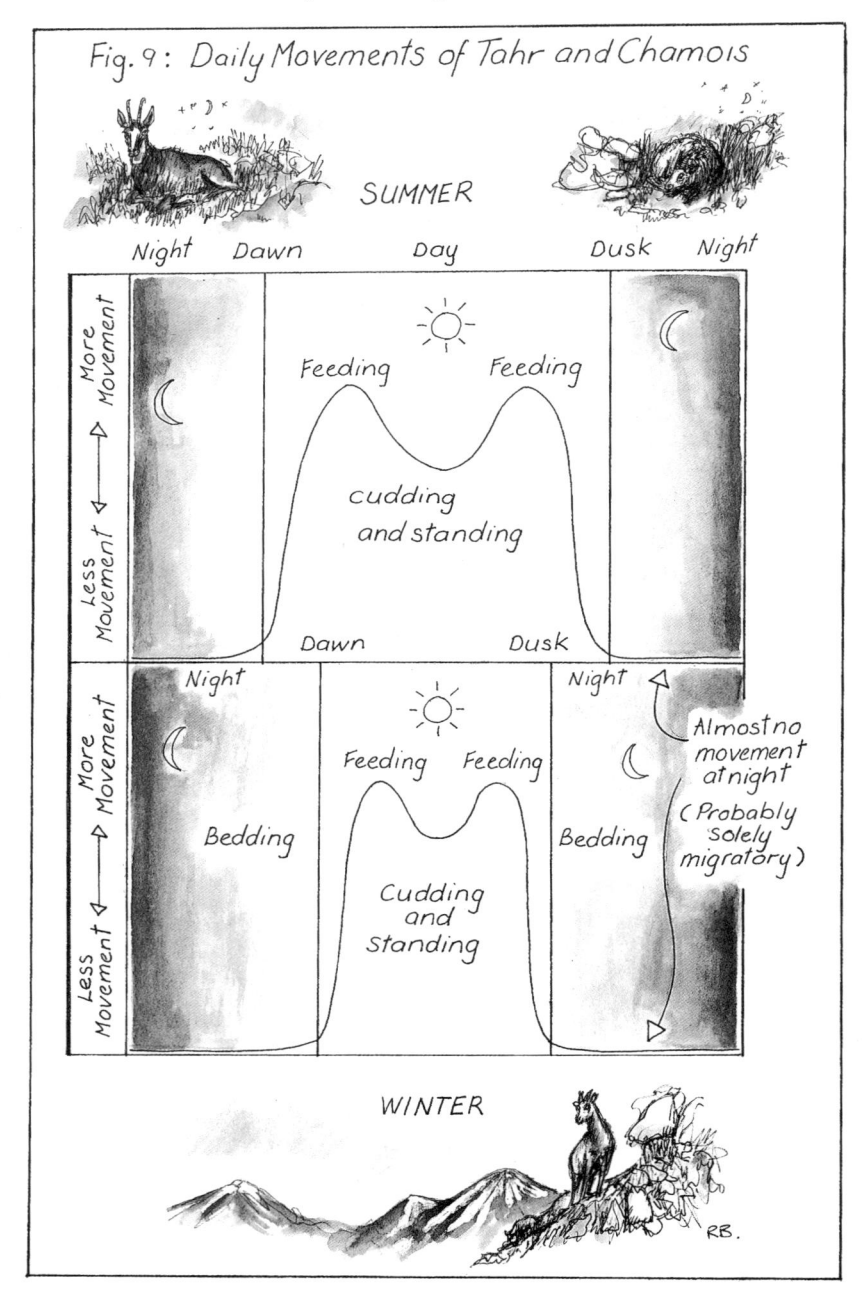

Fig. 9: Daily Movements of Tahr and Chamois

SUMMER

Night | Dawn | Day | Dusk | Night

More Movement ↔ Less Movement

Feeding — Feeding
Cudding and standing

Dawn — Dusk

Night | Night

Feeding — Feeding
Cudding and Standing

Bedding | Bedding

Almost no movement at night (Probably solely migratory)

WINTER

RB.

and culminate in the rut. On pp. 70–3 we describe these movements in more detail.

Day and night

As discussed, chamois are seldom mobile at night, except when they migrate seasonally or undergo nocturnal movements during the rut. They may also move at night if a storm blows up and they need to shift for shelter, or if they are disturbed by humans. Nonetheless, in most situations where New Zealand chamois have been studied, the animals have consistently been found bedded in the morning where they were last seen the night before.

Figure 9 shows variations of activity according to the angle of the sun. (You may find it interesting to compare this with the figure on page 18 of *Stalking the Seasons Round*, which shows activity variations by day and night for species of deer.) Although chamois and deer operate differently at night, there are similarities during the day. Both have peak movements around dawn and dusk, with activity decreasing in the hottest part of the day.

Since this graph was originally drawn, it has been found that feeding behaviour even more particularly follows the pattern of the graph. It has also been found that, as with red deer and other non-tropical deer, there is a general reduction in feeding activity in the winter months. Also, periods of bad weather in any season cause a slight decline in feeding and general activity.

Weather

Knowing how chamois behave in response to weather can be useful to the hunter. In calm, fine weather you can expect to find the herds thinly scattered about the feeding grounds; but where will they be during wind, rain or snow? And how will they react to weather changes? If you know the answers, you can often achieve success even on 'bad' days. We will now consider one by one the weather factors that influence chamois behaviour.

Winter versus summer coat

New Zealand chamois are transplanted animals existing in a climate different from the European continental climate in which they evolved. Broadly speaking, the European summers have an average temperature similar to New Zealand but show less day-to-day variation. European winters on the other hand are colder, with many clear, cold days and nights. Again, European winter days show less day-to-day variation than those here in New Zealand. The chamois coat is therefore evolved for conditions a little different from what they encounter here. It is thought that this mismatch of coat to environment gives rise to peculiarities of behaviour in New Zealand animals.

In summer, the chamois coat is about right for the average New Zealand conditions; however, conditions are more changeable than in European summers, with cold southerly storms possible at any time, perhaps quickly followed by hot sunny weather. In such variable summer conditions, New Zealand chamois are forced to take considerable time and effort to avoid overheating or getting too cold.

On very hot days the animals are prone to overheat and so, particularly at mid-day, seek out shady places under rock outcrops or in the bush. They may even be found lying in the odd patch of snow that has not yet melted from sites of particularly heavy winter accumulations. On these warm days, they are likely to be found at higher altitudes and on south-facing slopes. On colder days in summer the converse applies, and the animals will seek out warmer, north-facing basins that are often lower in altitude.

With the coming of winter, as the animals grow their heavy, dark winter coat that has evolved to keep them warm in the colder European winter, any problems of being too cold disappear. They can easily withstand the worst the New Zealand winter has to offer. However, in the transitional days before winter has started to bite, all the new-grown insulation may be an embarrassment, particularly to the bucks. In the Cupola Basin study area at Nelson Lakes National Park, chamois have been observed to move 300-500 metres higher immediately after their change into winter coat. This is quite the opposite of what we would expect.

Some scientists dispute this 'coat mismatch, hotter in winter' theory, and argue that the upward movements are because the animals seek out more sunlit and less shaded areas. But whatever the explanation, the results are the same — in some areas the animals are found higher during winter. There is also a similar dispute as to why tahr in some areas are found higher in winter.

Given that chamois are well suited to withstand the worst that the New Zealand winter can throw at them, what day-to-day factors do influence their movement?

Snow

Chamois in winter occupy smaller ranges than in summer. For example, a study was done on chamois in Basin Creek in the Southern Alps. In summer they had ranges averaging about 207 hectares, but in winter their average was 70 hectares.

While deep, soft snow acts as a physical barrier it does not ultimately limit the movements of chamois herds, as the spring migrations of the floater herds show. Chamois can travel well up on top of the snow when it is firmed by frost. This is due to the structure of their feet (see the photographs in the colour section). The cleaves are broader and rounder in outline, and thus less prone to sink into the snow. There are, however, times of exception, even for chamois...

In June of 1970 I was on my first winter alpine hunt in the Rangitata. From the riverbed I saw a lone animal high up walking purposefully across a south-facing, snow-covered basin. My mate and I started off to see if we could intercept it. Soon we were floundering in soft snow, but kept on. Travelling up a steep spur, we surmounted a low hill and there, not fifty metres away, was a tired chamois slowly making its way downhill on a parallel spur opposite. On seeing me, the animal was alarmed, but with its belly at times dragging in the deep snow it was not able to escape quickly and thus my friend was able to shoot a winter-coated mature buck. The moral of this tale is to keep a careful watch on snow conditions. This can enable you to stalk up on groups marooned in bad snow. FS

Apart from difficulties of travel, deep snow cover can cause other problems for chamois. A heavy snowfall over level or gently sloping grazing grounds of the high pastures covers up the vegetation and prevents them from grazing there. But on steeper faces such deep snow is more likely to slip or avalanche away, exposing the grasses again, and so it is to these areas that the animals head once the snows come in earnest. The highly agile chamois are able to graze even the steepest slopes.

Failing this, you can try searching two other types of ground. Firstly search the difficult broken bluff areas where small terraces hold growth that is protected from snow accumulation by wind or overhangs. Secondly, try the areas under bluffs adjacent to rock screes, where avalanching snow or frost-heaved rocks from above scoop off the snow burden, exposing potential grazing.

Having said this, a word of caution is needed. Steep places are dangerous, particularly in winter. They are even dangerous to the sure-footed chamois. Sometimes frozen chamois carcasses are to be found at the foot of favourite bluffs from where they have accidentally fallen or been knocked off by falling rocks or avalanche. Knowledge and practice of mountain craft greatly improves your chances of staying alive and unharmed.

Hunting chamois can take you into dangerous situations, and the snow makes it difficult to get around and cover the ground. What makes winter hunting worthwhile is the fact that chamois are more confined by snow and ice conditions. A reduction in range can result in a concentration of animals into one or two densely populated spots, and if you know where these are you can score. The reward is a trophy head bearing the impressive black winter skin with white and cream markings.

However, a word to the faint-hearted. If you are not willing to risk your health on the steep alpine places of winter, you may still be able to hunt chamois below the bush edge. Pick an area of your winter hunting grounds where there is an extensive, heavy blanket of snow. Hunt the upper bush edge below this. This is where the animals may be, driven by hunger to forage in the bush interior, particularly where palatable forage trees have been broken down by snow burden. Also, be sure to look carefully over any slips and open creekbeds within the bush: chamois are reluctant bush dwellers and open places within it attract them.

Always remember, when hunting the bush edge below a heavy snow burden on the tops above, you still need to have an eye to avalanche conditions. When given a good head start, boulders can bounce and hurtle quite some distance down into the forest. Likewise, snow avalanches can roar down and overwhelm whole areas of high-altitude forest. On the days when you spot chamois staying close in at the bases of bluffs, watch out — they are probably using the overhang as protection from imminent avalanche!

Wind

Chamois have a thick winter coat which traps body heat by holding warm air within its hairs. Like all fur-bearing animals, however, they are susceptible to the loss of this body heat by wind-chill. Thus, even chamois will seek shelter when the winter winds are strong and cold. Broken bluffs offer a good refuge. The rock chimneys in these bluffs can provide shelter from the winds blowing parallel to the rock face, and yet are not far from winter feeding areas below bluffs where avalanches and rock falls have exposed vegetation.

During the warmer weather, because of the problems we have already discussed, chamois will on occasion use the wind to keep cool. Wind is more common in both exposed places and at higher altitude. This is the reason for a general gaining of altitude in autumn when the animals change to winter coat.

Cloud and fog

Unfortunately for the hunter fog-bound at camp it appears chamois are active grazers in the mist. Probably they sense they are safe from prying hunters' eyes. This fact, at least, is widely reported from research on chamois in Europe. In New Zealand, fog seems to have stopped hunter and researcher alike.

Chamois in the wild have never been observed drinking water. It is thought they get all their moisture from the greenstuff they eat. Perhaps this is why they like it when the mist is down — grazing wet grass is the nearest thing they get to drinking water.

Trying to hunt in the mist is frustrating because you cannot see far to find animals and it is dangerous because it's dead easy to get lost or bluffed. Mist often blows in quickly — and can also lift quickly. In New Zealand's tempestuous weather system, clouds and fogbanks can disperse suddenly to reveal grazing animals, caught unawares. In chamois hunters' camps, the sudden lifting of the curtain of damp can trigger a mass exodus to the hunting grounds. Keep an eye out for the mist coming back again, though! Even familiar ground with its known landmarks often becomes strange and unknown when all is wrapped up in the cotton-wool of fog. When venturing out in such conditions the hunter should place temporary markers at close intervals along the route, to help find the way home if the fog returns.

Food and feeding behaviour

One of the big differences between New Zealand and Europe is that our alpine pastures are a poorer food source. As a result, the hunter here is unlikely to encounter large groups of chamois, and our chamois have larger range sizes. When reading about chamois in Europe it is important to bear this difference in mind. For example, a scientist talking about chamois in Switzerland says, 'It is astonishing how small an area bucks can graze for many hours.' Detailed studies in New Zealand, however, show that perhaps with the exception of a few choice spots in the height of summer, nothing could be further from the truth here. Chamois do have the ability to utilize a wide variety of grasses and shrubs, but in New Zealand they need to keep on the move throughout their range to pick out the good grazing when it is ready. In the more luxuriant and uniform pastures of Switzerland, movements of herds within their ranges often involve only a shift in altitude following the wave of seasonal growth as it moves up the mountainside.

In New Zealand, you can learn to predict the autumn 'coat-mismatch movement' (see p.60) and the migrations of the floater populations of chamois. However, movements of chamois in the course of their daily search for food are much less predictable. These movements vary according to what patches of what particular vegetation are found in an individual animal's range. Nonetheless, sufficient information is available to work out some useful rules of thumb.

In contrast to the situation when hunting deer, a detailed knowledge of individual plant species is less important for the chamois hunter as chamois eat a wider range of plants. Once a chamois has moved onto a particular type of feeding ground it will often remain there for a considerable time, perhaps only moving when forced to by weather or change of season. It is thus primarily a knowledge of these various types of alpine feeding grounds, where they occur and when they are used, that can help the hunter predict where the animals will be.

Types of alpine ground

Undisturbed chamois spend most of their time feeding in the open. This makes it relatively simple to study their feeding behaviour. An observer in a hide with powerful binoculars or a telescope can observe and record where they are eating and sometimes even what plants they are eating. A series of such observations made in New Zealand has built up a good picture of the way in which chamois utilise differing regions of mountain vegetation. (See Appendix 4.)

We will now look at the various alpine regions, starting from the highest and most barren and working down-slope. We will note plants of particular food value that are especially favoured by chamois. Fig. 10 shows the seasonal patterns of use of these regions.

High alpine barrens. These are places of mainly bare rock with just a few tenacious plants. They are completely covered by snow in winter and bear little of food value, although chamois are sometimes seen in these areas during winter travelling over the covering snow.

Fellfields and herbfields. Both these are high places above the tussock grasslands where there is just enough soil for herbs to grow. In fellfields the soil is thinner and the plant covering more sparse, often with areas of bare rock between. Such areas are only used by chamois during the peak summer growth periods. A plant group that is eaten by chamois and commonly grows in these regions is the easily recognized mountain daisies (*Celmisia* spp.). Other species eaten are less conspicuous such as the mountain snowberries (*Gaultheria* spp.).

Herbfields are also found in small islands within the lower alpine grassland areas, and here research indicates that they are important food sources for chamois on the alpine grasslands (see later).

Alpine grasslands. These are the familiar lands of waving tussock that occur above the tree-line and are covered by snow in winter. In between the tussocks, and at times forming whole areas in the tussock grasslands, are the highly favoured herb species which make this an important feeding zone for chamois throughout the year. In winter, the animals will use areas where the slope is enough for the snow covering to slip, exposing the vegetation beneath. Areas of grassland within bluff systems are particularly important. In summer, the more gently sloping zones are used, often as soon as they are free of winter snow.

In some areas, for example Cupola Basin in Nelson Lakes National Park, the tussock grasses themselves are used for food, particularly the short-bladed species *Poa colensoi* and the *Festuca* species. The longer-bladed, probably less preferred snow tussocks (*Chionochloa* spp.) are also used in some areas. With more detailed study of chamois feeding behaviour it has been increasingly realized that the intervening patches of herbs are probably more important to the chamois than the tussock itself. The herbs are possibly eaten on a year-round cycle as they ripen, along with a measure of the tussock grasses as well.

The following list of favoured herb species has been noted to be taken in the Avoca area of the Southern Alps.

Species probably favoured in spring and summer
Mountain buttercup (*Ranunculus foliosus*)
Snowberry (*Gaultheria depressa*)
Mountain daisies (*Celmisia* spp.)

In damper places:
Willow herb (*Epilobium* spp.)
Mountain gentians (*Gentiana* spp.)
Creeping pohuehue (*Muehlenbeckia axillaris*)

Species favoured in winter:
Pinatoro (*Pimelia prostrata*)
Creeping matipo (*Myrsine nummularis*)
Dish-leaved hebe (*Hebe pinguifolia*)

An area of tussock grassland may look from a distance as plain and uniform as a farmer's hay paddock, but this is deceptive: alpine communities are complex. Even in the most uniform-looking areas there will be an underlying lattice of herbs providing nourishment at different times. The diversity and range of these herbs, along with their varying ripening patterns, provides another reason for the wandering lifestyle of the New Zealand chamois.

Occasionally a more concentrated area of a particular food plant species will 'ripen' and the zone will be converged on by all the chamois in that area. This creates a temporary 'hot spot'. Research shows that range convergence of this type does not happen often, so for the hunter knowledge of these temporary areas is hard won. If you do find a seasonal concentration of animals in the same place year after year, a gut sample taken from a shot animal may enable you to work out which food plant they are seeking out. You could then possibly determine the extent of the area where this plant is common (you will often have to search under the tussocks to see them), and predict the recurrence of that hot spot in the next season.

Alpine shrublands These are the areas generally occurring below the alpine grasslands and above the forests. Usually called the leatherwood band or scrub zone by hunters, they are areas where woody interwoven shrubs grow, typically in dense thickets. Traversing such areas is usually tiresome and difficult. In some places alpine shrublands cover extensive zones; in others, where the beech forests open out directly onto the tussock, they are non-existent. Alpine scrub areas do not commonly provide much in the way of food for chamois, but are often used as concealment cover.

Chamois may move in and occupy alpine scrub regions for long periods when heavy hunting pressure disturbs their life in the open. Scrub is also sometimes used by chamois when winter snows invade alpine grasslands.

Although there is little in the way of food plants beneath the leatherwood canopy, there are sometimes small islands of alpine herbfield or grassland in the scrub belt and these are likely to provide sustenance for chamois when they are holed up in concealment country. Often chamois can be seen from a distance feeding these small open areas, but it can be extremely difficult to get close enough for a shot — to say nothing of finding the animal afterwards.

Forested areas Surveys in the Avoca Valley show a low incidence of sightings in the bush. This contrasts with the observations of hunters, who report numbers of chamois living in forests, particularly in areas exposed to high helicopter hunting pressure. However, the tallies in the Avoca survey may be artificially low, because in forest the animals are more difficult to spot.

When chamois do inhabit forest and shrublands, there is evidence they may eat similar food to that consumed by deer, in particular broadleaved *Coprosma* species. In addition, they also seem able to eat the tougher vegetation, for example *Hebe* and *Dracophyllum*.

Montane grasslands These are the lower tussocklands, at altitudes below 1000 metres. They often contain areas of matagouri scrub and are dominated by the native tussock *Festuca novae-zelandiae* which is thought to be unpalatable to chamois. For this reason, chamois do not generally favour the montane grasslands, using them only in the winter months when snow covers their preferred territories. When forced down onto these low grasslands, chamois will seek out the more palatable introduced pasture grasses such as *Agrostis*. Even then, they will only use the areas of higher elevation, avoiding places where farm stock are held.

Preferred food plants: the importance of rumen studies

The plants listed in the above section are guideline examples taken from the studies of C.M.H. Clarke. These listings of species give some idea of favoured plants in each vegetation zone and are thus a starting point on where to hunt. However, knowing the preferred plants is only one side of the coin; the other is to gain some idea of the actual day-to-day quantity of herbage of the various species eaten, and thus some idea of what the animals' main diet is. Only this will give you a clear indication of what vegetation type the animal spends the most time eating — regardless of what dainty morsels it most prefers. By studying this, the hunter is able to get a more 'average' idea of what sort of greenery the animal will be typically found in.

See Fig.10, which is based on the rumen studies of J. Parke, car-

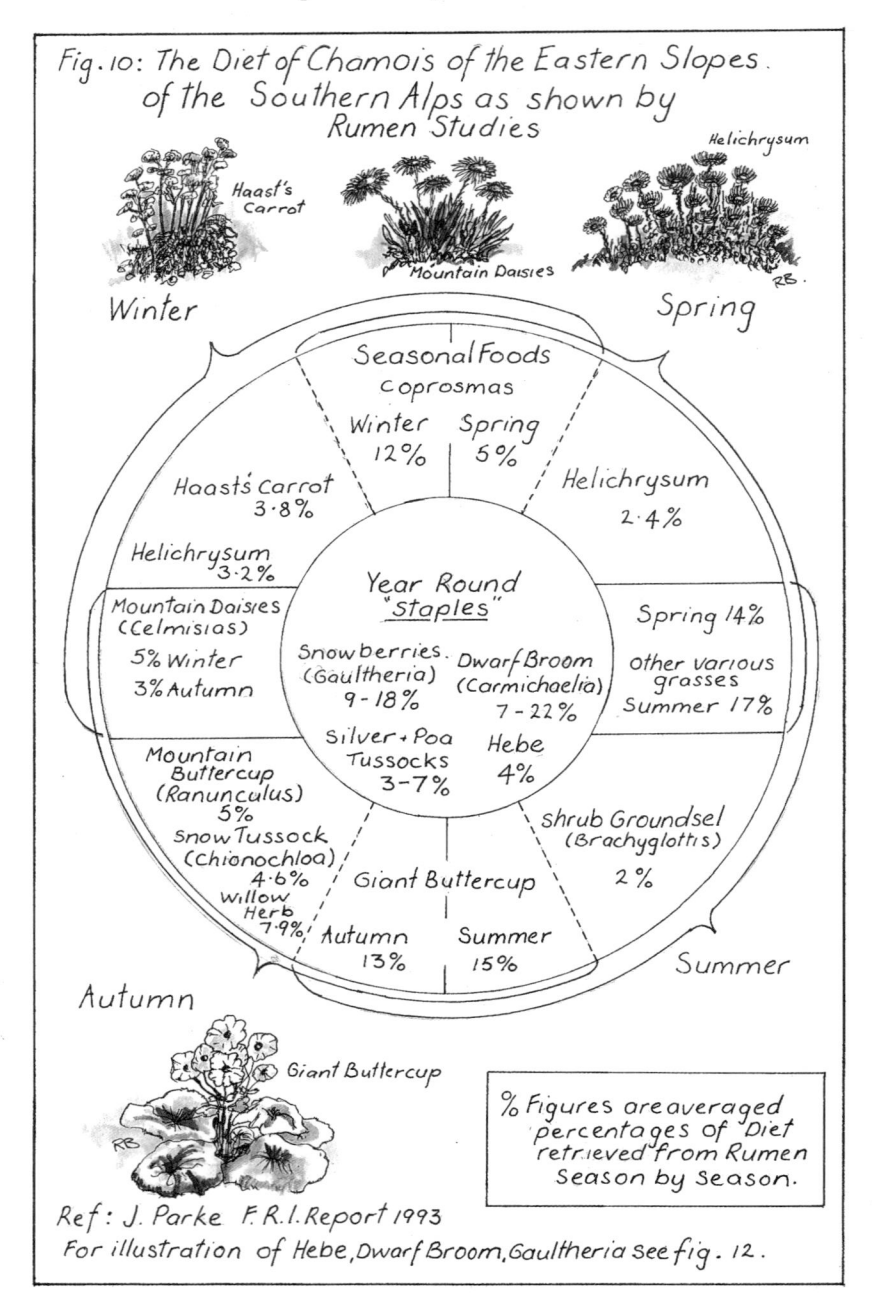

Fig. 10: The Diet of Chamois of the Eastern Slopes of the Southern Alps as shown by Rumen Studies

Winter — Haast's Carrot
Spring — Mountain Daisies, Helichrysum
Autumn — Giant Buttercup

Seasonal Foods

Coprosmas
- Winter 12%
- Spring 5%

Helichrysum 2.4%

Spring 14%
Other various grasses Summer 17%

shrub Groundsel (Brachyglottis) 2%

Giant Buttercup
- Autumn 13%
- Summer 15%

Mountain Buttercup (Ranunculus) 5%
Snow Tussock (Chionochloa) 4.6%
Willow Herb 7.9%

Mountain Daisies (Celmisias)
- 5% Winter
- 3% Autumn

Helichrysum 3.2%

Haast's Carrot 3.8%

Year Round "Staples"

- Snowberries (Gaultheria) 9–18%
- Dwarf Broom (Carmichaelia) 7–22%
- Silver + Poa Tussocks 3–7%
- Hebe 4%

% Figures are averaged percentages of Diet retrieved from Rumen Season by season.

Ref: J. Parke F.R.I. Report 1993
For illustration of Hebe, Dwarf Broom, Gaultheria see fig. 12.

ried out in 1993. Note particularly that the year-round 'staples' which together account for between 49% and 37% of the diet in a given season do not include *Chionocloa* tussocks. It is also interesting to see that of the available grasses, the *Chionocloa* snow tussocks are least preferred, being only grazed significantly in autumn when the total intake from the staples is at its lowest (27%). *Poa* grasses and the silver tussock are preferred above *Chionocloa*, and are the only species of grass grazed significantly year-round.

Apart from the staples, it is notable that different woody plants and herbs are grazed during different seasons. Presumably the factors influencing these seasonal patterns of consumption are whether the plants are ripe, whether they are accessible in snow and whether they are in the seasonal range shifts of the animals.

Competition with other game species

It was previously noted that chamois grazing lower-altitude montane grasslands avoid areas where farm stock are held. Only recently has it been realized that the presence of other game species has a particular influence over the places that chamois frequent, and thus their diet. Broadly speaking, these changes are brought about by competition for suitable grazing and browsing sites. This is not to say the competition is direct, i.e., that one species literally chases the other off a disputed patch. It is in all probability more likely to be indirect, where one species is simply better at getting the food from that site and thus starves the other out. However, no one knows for sure. What is known, however, is that chamois are particularly likely to be 'competed out' by red deer, nanny tahr and, on occasion, goats.

Firstly, it appears that chamois, when under competition from another species on the tops, will expand their range by moving well down into the bush, where they graze slips and even river flats. They are especially likely to do this when there is also the pressure of helicopter hunting. However, they can only make this move down-slope successfully in areas where there are very low numbers of deer in the bush; otherwise the deer provide too strong competition for chamois on these lower grazing sites.

The lesson for the hunter is that in areas where deer numbers are very low the chamois hunter should hunt not only the tops but also areas lower in the bush, paying particular attention to the grassy flats and slips. These are the same places red deer are drawn to in spring, but chamois can be expected to graze there year-round. This hunting strategy is likely to be particularly profitable when there is helicopter hunting pressure encouraging the animals to seek cover, or a good snow burden covering up grazing sites on the higher pastures.

In some areas, goats (distant cousins of the chamois) are also present in the lower places. It seems that when chamois and goats live together on the same low country places they divide up the slips between them so the hunter will either encounter exclusively goats on a slip or only chamois. Here it appears that owing to their closer kinship the competition is more even, the chamois sometimes holding their own.

An even more complex situation occurs where chamois and tahr inhabit the same regions. Scientists have found that chamois are 'competed out' by nanny tahr. Thus if you see nanny tahr, you should not expect to see chamois in the area (and vice-versa). On the other hand, chamois seem to be able to live alongside the bachelor herds of bull tahr that are found in some valleys, particularly in spring and summer. In this case, however, there is a difference between what the chamois are eating when they are living alongside the tahr and what they are eating after the tahr depart for the nanny grounds in the rut. It seems that a sort of 'truce' is reached whereby the bull tahr concentrate on one set of plants and chamois move over a little to concentrate on another. Scientists call this niche division. However, this is only a temporary situation, and when the tahr leave the chamois revert to eating from the full range of plants. Apart from its scientific curiosity value, this finding has some value to hunters. If you spot a herd of tahr sharing an area with chamois, you can be reasonably confident that you have found a herd of bull tahr.

The rut

During April, May and June great changes take place on the chamois hunting grounds; not only are the summer pastures lost, but the herds start responding to the call of the rut. Usually by the onset of April the first sprinklings of winter snow lie on the high ridges and the migrant male and female populations are leaving their summer foraging grounds, or have already left. By May, the males have adopted a foot-loose, wandering lifestyle, seeking out females wherever they may be. The migrant females, it is thought, head for traditional but transient breeding sites.

The permanent populations of course stay put, but being predominantly female they are highly attractive to the wandering bucks

Hunting chamois

Fig. 11: Chamois Behaviour During the Rut
(Occurs in Mixed Herds)
Male in his own territory usually claims mate

<u>Primarily Rutting Behaviour Male to Female</u>

Head Movements

Side to Side

Up and Down

Body Shake

Neck parallel to ground

Head up Lateral Humped Display
(sometimes may use Low Stretch)
✗ No Twist
✗ No Kick (stamps foreleg instead)
✓ Horning of Vegetation

<u>Aggressive Interactions</u>
(More common during Rut)
Female to Male
Male to Male

Humped Approach → Lateral Display
Head up and Low stretch
Head down.

CONTACT

clashing
(extremely rare)

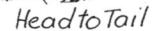

THREAT

plus Parallel Walk
Threat Bounding
Horning
Chasing

Head to Tail

which begin to invade. Male chamois which live in permanent areas also adopt a more roaming lifestyle at this time. Thus the whole male population, except for the odd aged, sedentary male, is on the move. To the hunter, this means a better chance of an encounter. The rut is thus a good time for trophy hunting.

The rut peaks in late May to early June. At this time chamois bear a bigger than usual lump on the top of their head just behind the base of their horns. The males also acquire a musky odour. The lump and odour are caused by the enlargement of the post-cornual or 'rutting' gland. The enlargement is triggered by hormonal changes in the animal and these hormonal changes are in turn triggered by the changes in day-length that occur as the autumn nights grow longer.

The ability to distinguish bucks from nannies is particularly handy during the rut, because then, more than at any other time, male and females are found in mixed company. The enlargement of the post-cornual gland in bucks can sometimes be seen at a distance by careful observation of the head. Also, a slight difference in horn form can also be used (see p. 76 and the photographs in the colour section). Nevertheless, even using these two methods together, distinguishing the sexes by looking at the head end is difficult. Often it is better to look at the animal's belly for the pizzle (only males have one!) and the 'soil patch'. This is a dark area on the underbelly of bucks extending forward from the pizzle. It is caused by the buck directing his hormone-laden urine stream upward, deliberately soiling himself in the same way as deer in the rut. In chamois this is sometimes done in a peculiar manner. The animal stands slightly crouched with neck parallel to the ground and urinates in this position whilst shaking his back, sides and whole body, to spray urine on his underside. This manoeuvre is termed the 'body shake' and is only seen in chamois.

Buck rivalry

Unlike stags, chamois bucks in New Zealand do not exhibit an overly active rivalry. Lower population numbers in New Zealand enable each buck to form a small harem, probably without the need to fight other males. In Europe, in areas where fertile conditions and hospitable country make for high population densities, fighting between rival males does take place. In more rugged and less fertile areas of Europe, however, there is a wider separation of smaller numbers and a quiet rut — as there is in New Zealand.

This low-energy mating behaviour of males is typical of the goat family. The goat-like horns of chamois are carried by both sexes and are poorly designed for pushing or goring contests. They are thought to function more as indicators of rank and for defence against predators, rather than as weapons for the rut.

A kinship of chamois to tahr is revealed in the typical confrontation between two rival chamois bucks (see Fig. 11). Each buck stands side on to the other and fluffs out his mane and upper body hairs in a display designed to make him appear large, powerful and intimidating. Often rival bucks will stand stock-still and broadside on to each other — sometimes with raised muzzles — remaining thus for 15 minutes or more until one of them, sensing that he is outclassed, will break and run. Sometimes he is then chased off by the victor. The resultant chase takes place at high speed either up hill or down and is an impressive display of the fitness and agility of buck chamois.

Other displays of rivalry have been recorded overseas. They include a head-down, hump-backed display very similar to that of bull tahr, bounding towards a rival in a threatening manner, and head-to-tail circling by rival males. (See Fig. 11.)

Generally speaking, both buck and doe chamois are naturally curious, particularly during the rut, and will often investigate something which is unusual. A half-concealed hunter can even, on occasion, cause a chamois to walk towards him, particularly when on the same level as the animal, or above.

Mating

You will be lucky to witness a buck contest. More likely the only evidence you will see that the rut is underway is observing a single buck in company with a single doe. Sometimes you may see a buck and two does. This is in all probability a family group of a doe and her six-month-old female kid. The kid is unlikely to conceive even if mating does take place, as it seems the earliest a female chamois can become fertile is 18 months. In more remote, undisturbed areas with higher chamois numbers, more extended maternal family groups of three animals may be held by a buck. The third animal is likely to be the previous year's female kid, now 18 months old and capable of breeding.

The onset of mating is also quiet. The buck seems merely to join up with a solitary female or female family group and follow them around, displaying in a similar manner to that used to repel rival bucks (in particular the 'low stretch' posture where the neck is held low and the head held muzzle up). He waits for them to come on heat, while standing on guard against male intruders. He will at intervals sniff at the hindquarters of the nanny, causing her to urinate. The buck then tests the urine by smell to see if the nanny is in her fertile period, at the same time curling back his lip in the 'showing flehmen' posture (see *Red Deer in New Zealand*).

From time to time he may mark shrubs nearby by rubbing them with secretions from his post-cornual gland. In this way the buck may stay in company with the nanny group for two weeks — possibly longer if he has missed the first nanny's fertile period.

The nanny group for its part seems to have the same outward indifference to the whole process as do red deer hinds. The nannies simply stay with their normal daily routine before and after mating. They allow the buck to mount only when they are at the peak of their fertile period. They will, however, when the occasion deserves it, vigorously repel the advances of immature or inferior bucks.

Breaking up of mating groups and calving

By mid-June most mating groups will have broken up. The animals either return to their own areas of permanent range or migrate separately to their temporary winter pastures. Chamois bucks usually maintain good condition during the mating period, even though they feed little during the rut. This is probably because they expend relatively little energy during their fighting or herding activities.

The gestation period (the time from conception to birth) is five-and-a-half to six months. Chamois kids are normally born between late October and early December. For some migrant nannies the crossing of high mountains to reach winter pastures in the west will mean staying there not only until the birth of their kid but until late December when the spring thaw enables their newborn kids to negotiate the return passage. Other migrant nannies will return east again sometime before late November and give birth to their kids on the eastern ranges.

The nature of the beast: anatomy

Differences between bucks and nannies

When New Zealand and European chamois are compared, the New Zealand animals are found to be somewhat smaller. Listed below are some data on body measurements for mature New Zealand chamois. The main points to note are that there is little difference between

New Zealand averages		
	Male	*Female*
Gutted weight (kg)	17–25	13–21
Liveweight (kg):	25–45	19–35
Shoulder height (mm)	650–900	600–800
Body length (mm)	1180–1300	1150–1210
Arawhata River (South Westland), 1970-71, late colonizing phase		
Average measurements		
Gutted weight (kg)	21.4	20.4
Body length (mm)	1180	1204
Horn length (mm)	223.4	214.0
Avoca River (mid-Canterbury) 1975-78, established population		
Average measurements		
Gutted weight (kg)	16.4	13.8
Body length (mm)	1246	1209
Horn length (mm)	225.1	184.3

male and females, but that there is a large variation within each range. For example the weight of a chamois buck can vary from 25 to as much as 45 kg.

When hunting chamois, the similarity in size between the two sexes makes it difficult to tell them apart. Earlier, we discussed two differences that occur during the breeding season (the post-cornual gland on the skull and the pizzle soiling of the male). The best method available in all seasons is probably to be found in the structure of the horns. In the males the horns are, when viewed front on, parallel up to the base of the 'hook'. At the start of the hook they begin to diverge and thus tilt a little away from one another. In the female, not only are the horns lighter, but they tilt more to create a greater distance between the hooks.

Beside horns, other differences are that the female is more lightly built, the winter coat of the male is darker, and the female adopts a semi-squatting posture when urinating. They are still difficult to tell apart in the field and even experienced hunters occasionally shoot nannies, mistaking them for bucks.

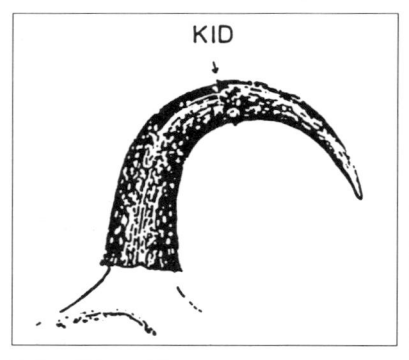

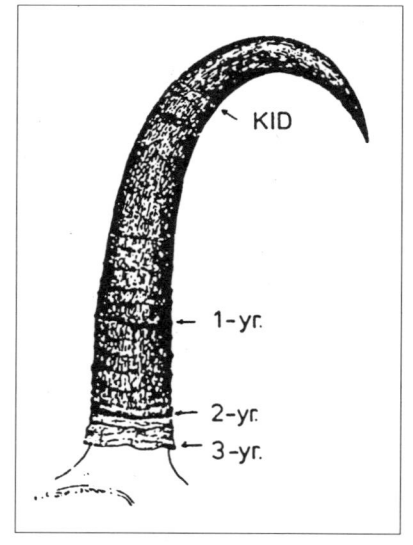

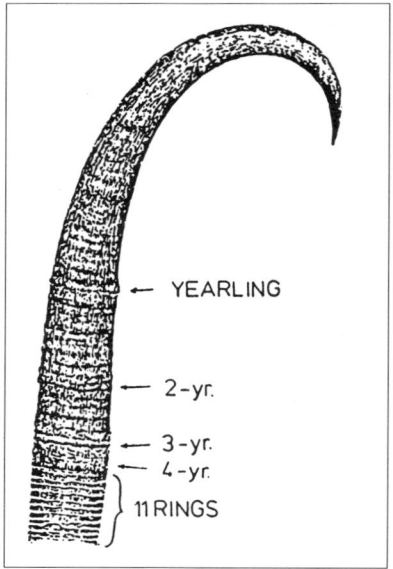

Fig. 12: Horn growth in Austrian chamois. Above left: Horn of a chamois yearling with two growth segments. The length of this animal's yearling segment is unusually long. Left: Three-year-old chamois male. The animal has two longer segments after that of the yearling. Above: Fifteen-year-old chamois male. The sequence of longer segments up to the age of four years has been marked with an arrow. Thereafter follow 11 "millimetre rings". From Lovari (1985), The Biology and Management of Mountain Ungulates.

Trophies

The chamois summer coat is red-brown, and lighter, with shorter hairs, than the brown-black winter coat. Both these coats make good trophies. Chamois skins are particularly durable. Their hair is finer than that of deer and not as easily broken by hard use. They even last a long time under hard use as floor mats.

Once a skin or two has been obtained, trophy horns become the over-riding reason many hunters continue to hunt chamois (although the meat is an acceptable goal for some). Chamois and all goats belong to the Bovidae family of animals in which, unlike deer which shed their antlers, the horns stay for life and grow more each year.

The older the beast is, the bigger are its horns. The horns increase considerably in length each year for the first two to three years, then the annual increase is just the small addition of a ring of growth at the horn's base. These rings can sometimes be counted to age the animal. In Fig. 12, we show a set of European chamois horns and their pattern of growth.

In spring and summer the animals are feeding heavily and laying down fat reserves for the demands of the rut and the winter ahead. During this time of plentiful food, horn growth occurs. When there is a break to this good nutrition, for example in the winter, horn growth stops. It is this stop-and-start that creates the growth rings. (However, in New Zealand conditions there is less seasonal variation in food supply than on the European continent, and so our chamois have less pronounced growth rings that are not as easy to count as those illustrated.) In New Zealand heads there is, nevertheless, a clear relationship between horn length and age. There is evidence that the annual horn is greater where there is better-quality food year round. (See also Appendix 1.)

There are perhaps two things you might look for when selecting an area in which to hunt for trophies. Firstly, it needs a good food supply. Consequently an area with a low population is best. Secondly, you have a better chance of finding mature animals where hunting pressure is light.

Unfortunately, it is not quite that simple. In some areas with poor food supplies the animals grow bigger than average. They are, however, leaner — as one would expect. This situation, for example, occurs in the Avoca River catchment. The table on p. 75 shows body length, carcass weight and horn length data for Avoca River and Arawhata River chamois (the latter is a more fertile area.) It can be seen that, in line with the poorer food supply, carcass weights are lower in the Avoca area — but body length is larger and the males have longer horns. Nevertheless, within the Arawhata population the females have on average larger horns than the Avoca females. This is all rather perplexing. Perhaps horn size in males is more influenced by genetics than food supply, but in females it is simply a question of food supply.

There is also an alternative explanation. It is well known that when new country is being colonized, animals there are considerably larger than those in long-established populations. This is because of the access the new migrants have to virgin vegetation. Also, unfortunately, when an area is being colonized, a sparse population arising from a few initial exploring animals is more likely to interbreed. Perhaps this higher rate of interbreeding somehow affects horn size in the Arawhata area.

It is not surprising in the light of all this that horn-length variation in New Zealand is not fully understood. However, when selecting an area in which to search for that special prize trophy, as well as considering the effects of nutrition and hunting pressure, you probably need to consider the size characteristics of the herd and whether the area has pockets of recent colonization.

Field sign

In areas where chamois occur along with other species, such as deer and tahr, it is worthwhile to learn to distinguish the trail of chamois.

The signs that chamois and deer leave behind in their bedding areas are also different. Chamois take after the common goat when selecting and using bedding areas. They frequent habitual shelter spots located hard-up against rocky outcrops or under overhangs. Here they often have scooped out bedding areas that are deeper than those deer make (as well as being found in a different situation). Not only this, but close to the beds are often found 'latrine areas' where large numbers of chamois pellets (slightly smaller and longer than those of red deer) are found. It is quite the opposite situation with deer, which never seem to deposit pellets near their resting and cudding areas — they prefer to void them when feeding or travelling.

Their senses

The eyes of chamois are more prominent, and larger in proportion to the size of the head than those of deer. This gives us a hint of the fact that to this animal the sense of vision is paramount and well developed. For this reason you should avoid walking along ridge crests. Instead, walk below the crest wherever possible. When hunting along a ridge, stay on the side that is less likely to hold animals. Walk around the top of the basin that you have thoroughly searched for chamois while positioning yourself for the next basin on the other side. Wherever possible stay on the downwind side.

Take extreme care crossing ridge crests. Either cross in the lee of a skyline shrub or rock or, in the case of an open razor-back, crawl. Spend long periods glassing from concealed positions before moving on. When chamois are lying in the inky shade of a rock in bright summer conditions they can be very difficult to spot. You may not know they are there until they move out and begin grazing — or running off because they spotted you!

In snow, look first for tracks, then for animals, and at the same time keep an ear out for sounds of chamois. A rock crashing down a slope may simply have been loosened by frost heave, or it could have been disturbed by a probing hoof. You can miss hearing the characteristic high pitched alarm whistle in a wind or at a distance if you are not listening for it, especially in windy conditions.

Although chamois have great eyesight, they have one particular weakness. Even in areas hunted by helicopters, they are likely to be alert for danger only coming up from below or around the side. Thus they are vulnerable to the foot-shooter hunting down from above. Even after a shot has been fired, provided you keep still and the wind is in your face, they often have difficulty in working out that they are being shot at from above.

As we have said, in spite of their great reliance on eyesight, chamois have a keen sense of smell and on this account you need to take care as to your windage. Always consider which way the wind is blowing — in particular you need to be aware of the effects of catabatic winds (see p. 25).

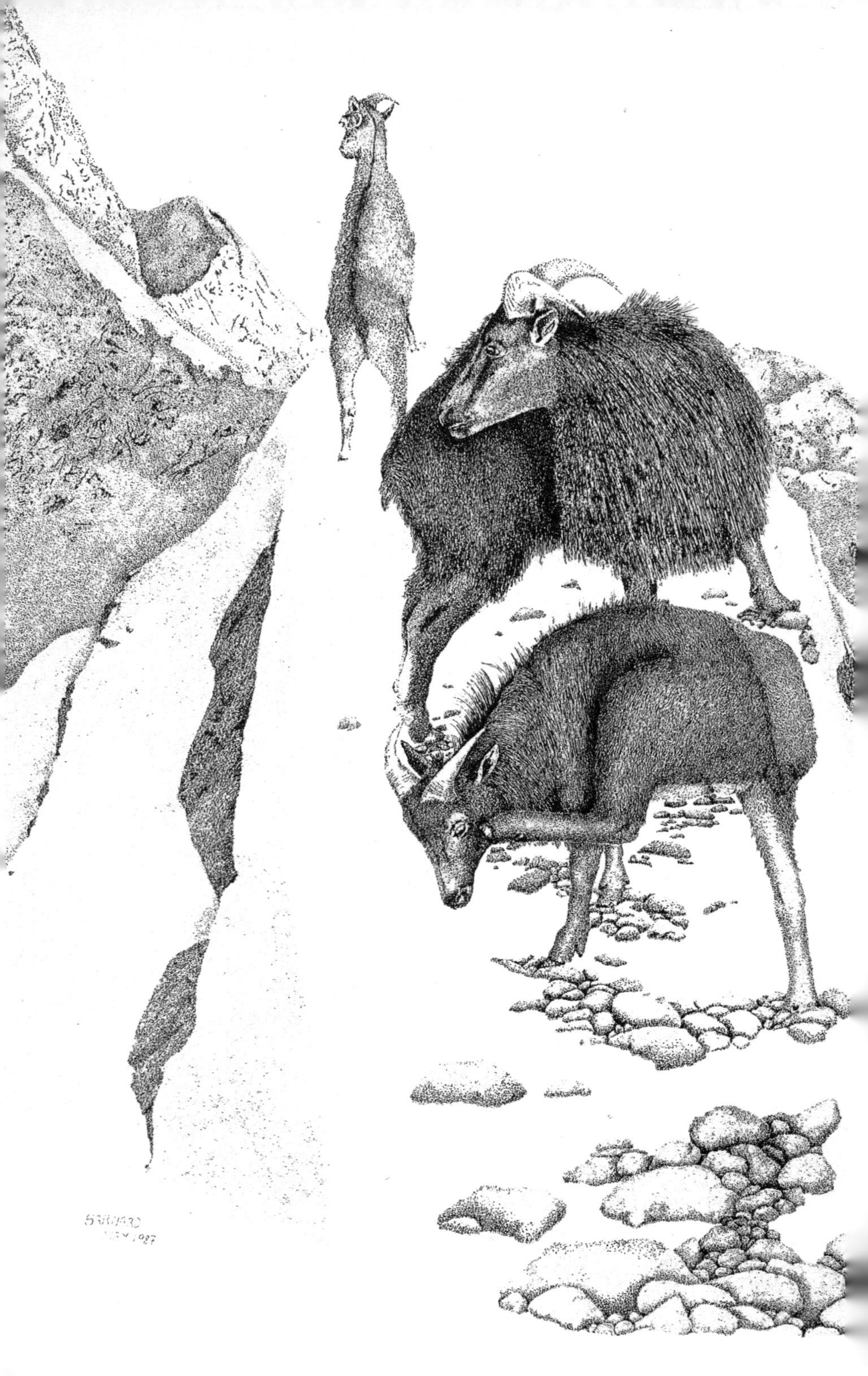

Tahr

*What have you seen on the summits, the peaks that
plunge their icy heads into space?
What draws you trembling to blind altars of rock
where man cannot linger?*

From *The Estate* by Charles Brasch

4
Hunting tahr

I enjoyed being a schoolboy because of the many holidays in which I was able to go hunting. When I left school in 1970 I didn't want to go to work, as most jobs only had a few weeks' holiday a year. Universities had more holidays. My home town was Hastings, but in my mind there were only two universities to choose from: Otago and Canterbury. This is because they were the only two located in the same island as tahr. I had never been to the South Island in my life, but I had read about tahr. In fact, I read everything I could about tahr. To me they were the ultimate hunting challenge. I chose Canterbury because it was not quite as far away from home as Otago. Within a month of being there I was on my first tahr hunting trip.

It was a three-day weekend and a new-found hunting mate and I drove the long straight roads out of Christchurch. Then we twisted and turned on shingle roads through the foothills before we parked near where two wide riverbeds met. One of them was called the Clyde, and up it we lurched, carrying packs and rifles, hopping from boulder to boulder for hours. We stopped at a hut called Watchdog Hut, and we were indeed tired dogs that night.

Behind the hut is a tall shingle scree leading to a high saddle. Early next morning my mate said, 'Come on, I'll show you an easy way to find tahr. We'll climb that big shingle scree.' Who was I to argue? So up that ladder of shattered rocks we toiled. The work had me sucking gulps of clear frost-tinged air as we strained upwards. Gigantic up-thrusts of rock towered ahead and alongside. A long river in flowing ribbons streamed out below. I was a North Islander and this was my first experience of the huge mountain country of our Southern Alps.

We disturbed a band of chamois along the way. They trailed off across the shingle scree above and into a bluff system on our right. They appeared to be only nannies and kids. In any case, chamois could wait. It was tahr I was after.

Hunting tahr

Two hours after leaving the hut we were at the top and gingerly peering over the rim of a saddle, looking across into a tussock basin. In the basin were tahr — at least 30, perhaps 50! They were nannies and kids for the most part, with some immature males. I had never seen a live tahr before, and now, suddenly, there was a mob of them. The closest ones were less than 100 metres away. A shot rang out from me — or my equally eager mate. As a group the tahr fled. They ran straight to the bluff that falls away below the basin. It overlooks Cattle Stream, 500 metres below. They were suddenly gone, and none of them were dead.

We ran across the basin and then gingerly looked over the edge. There, not 20 metres below, across a small gut and under an overhang was a tahr. We shot at it. Then we saw others. Despite being shot at, the tahr were reluctant to move; yet they had been so fleet of foot just five minutes before.

Walking around the bluff edge we found more, likewise 'sheltering'. We shot quite a few; I don't recall how many — maybe half a dozen. However, there was only one that, using all my courage, I could climb down to. It was a young bull kid. I skinned him with pride. Here was a real tahr, my first tahr. I still have his skin twenty years later. The fine young hairs have worn well, even though it has often been used as a floor mat.

Those tahr felt most unsafe on the basin, especially after the rifle shot. But tucked in the bluff system below, they stood huddled and waiting. Thousands of years of surviving avalanches had produced a genetic imprint: an instinctive urge to head for bluffs and shelter under overhangs in times of danger.

This was a marvellous introduction to alpine hunting, and I had plenty more holidays marked on the calendar ahead. FS

Any hunter who has seen the magnificent sight of a 100-kg bull tahr standing silhouetted against a rugged mountain backdrop is likely to agree that this is the ultimate quarry for the New Zealand hunter. Not only is the bull tahr an impressive sight, he has a remarkable ability to travel through the roughest terrain with consummate ease. This ability, coupled with the fact that he spends a considerable part of his life frequenting barren snow-covered heights, makes for hard hunting. Hunters who choose tahr as their quarry will be drawn into country that tests their mountaineering skills to the utmost. With such a hunting challenge presented by this animal, there is small wonder then that hunters have a ready will to fight the political battles needed to preserve the remnants of this mighty game herd.

In today's conditions of low numbers on steep terrain, the hunter who possesses an understanding of the animals' movements in varying conditions and seasons greatly increases the chances of securing a trophy. In this chapter we will consider the fundamentals in the same manner as we did for chamois, breaking down the complex picture into its parts, then drawing it together.

In the course of this account of tahr, you are likely to be struck by the numerous similarities in behaviour between chamois and tahr. In spite of the considerable differences in appearance the two are quite closely related. As we have already seen, chamois are from the group of animals called rock goats or goat/antelopes. Tahr are considered to be a halfway point between the rock-goat and the true goats (of which the common New Zealand wild goat is an example). We will discuss the finer points of distinction between tahr and chamois and their relevance to the hunter. Here, as an introduction to the beast, we make the point that tahr and chamois are both goat-like species, and as such exhibit behaviour patterns similar to the common feral goat. For example, tahr have a liking for rocky outcrops; they have a preference for resting places in the shelter of overhangs; and they have a habit of shedding droppings in these resting places. There are also other similarities, as we shall see later.

Although tahr are similar to goats, they are not true goats. There are marked biological differences between the two. For example, they are not able to interbreed as they have different numbers of chromosomes.

Movements of tahr

Like other members of the goat family, tahr hardly move at night. In fact they are so sedentary at night that scientists who observed their movements in a study in the Godley River area were able to pick up individual animals at first light within a few metres of where they had last seen them at sunset the night before. The hunter can do likewise.

New Zealand and overseas studies show that during the day tahr have a characteristic pattern of behaviour (see fig. 13). Peak feeding and movement occurs at dawn and dusk and the middle of the day is spend resting and cudding their relatively indigestible food. The basic daily movement pattern for tahr can therefore be described as follows. On rising from their overnight bedding sites a daily journey

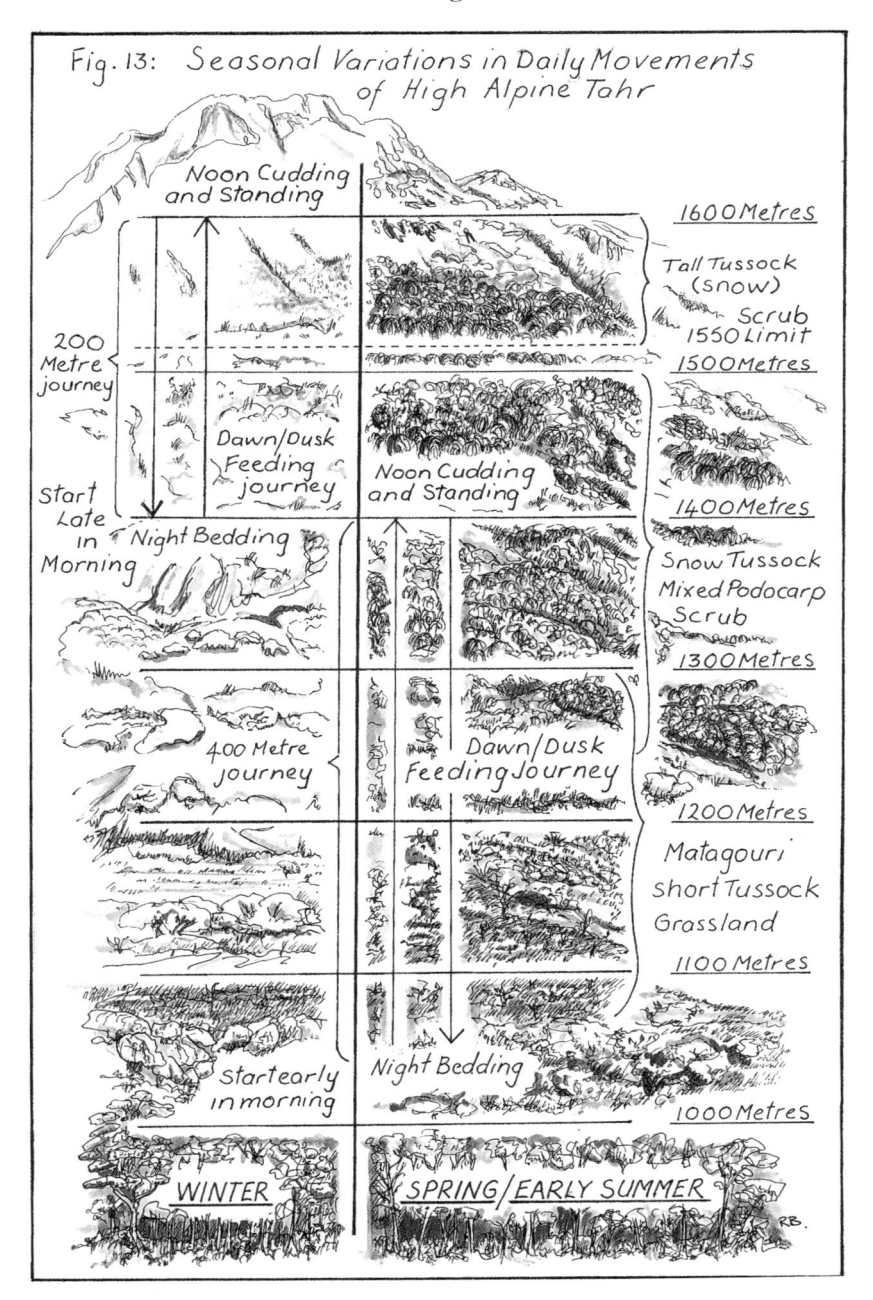

Fig. 13: Seasonal Variations in Daily Movements of High Alpine Tahr

is undertaken to and from a daytime resting place. The animals feed as they go. The amount of ground covered and the amount of feeding that takes place on the morning and afternoon journeys varies according to the season and the weather. We discuss the details of these variations later.

Temperature effects

Just as some of the movements of chamois arise from the fact that they possess a coat which is designed for colder conditions than exist in New Zealand, some scientists believe a similar situation exists in tahr.

Caughley, writing about tahr in Central Nepal, concluded that their natural habitat was between 3900 metres and 5300 metres. In New Zealand, careful year-round studies show that our animals live at altitudes of between only 1000 metres and 1700 metres.

Even allowing for the temperature differences arising from the fact that New Zealand is further away from the equator, it seems that our New Zealand tahr are forced to live in a warmer climate than their natural habitat — especially in winter. It is not surprising, then, to learn that in one New Zealand study tahr were observed to remain at higher altitudes in the winter and late autumn than they did in summer. In New Zealand, it seems, these animals, like chamois, are disadvantaged by the high insulative properties of their winter coat. They move to higher and colder places when bearing winter coat. In this study, they were found at 1550 metres at noon on a winter's day, descending to 1400 metres in the cool of dusk. Conversely, in the spring and summer, when in lighter coat, they were found between 1300 and 1400 metres in the warm mid-day period, descending at dusk as low as 1000 metres.

This, then, is the first pattern of movement you should recognize: the animals are likely to be found higher in winter than in summer. In winter particularly, they will climb to areas well above the vegetation line and remain in these wildernesses of rock and snow for long periods. Some scientists argue that the upward movement is, as with chamois, to move into areas of greater sunlight — away from the shadowy valleys. This does not, however, explain why the animals often stand on windy ridge crests at these higher elevations. In any event, hunting animals in these situations demands a high degree of mountaineering skill.

The fact that year-round bulls possess a heavier coat than nannies is a possible explanation for the important fact that at all seasons except the rut the bulls tend to be found at slightly higher altitudes than the nannies. Possibly they need that extra bit of wind and cold. At times the separation of the groups is only a few metres in height; on other occasions it can be hundreds of metres. The message is that if you spot a group of females, look higher up for the males — except during the rut.

Appetite regulation

There is good evidence that an appetite regulation mechanism exists in tahr, as in deer and chamois. This reduces the appetite in times of food shortage so that the animals do not waste energy foraging for scanty food supplies. In one New Zealand study it was shown that in winter the animals spent 20% less time per day feeding than during the summer months. The extra time was spent resting.

As we have seen, tahr rest during the middle period of the day, with dawn and dusk being the main times of feeding activity. (See Fig. 13.) In winter, feeding periods are shorter and the resting period is longer. In winter, then, you are less likely to intercept the animals as they move and feed, and more likely to spot them as they rest. Also, in winter these resting places are typically on the barren, open and highest places that they inhabit at any time of the year (see p. 86). If you wish to intercept the animals on their feeding journeys, there is a shorter period of time at the beginning and end of the day in which to do it. Also, on particularly cold frosty winter mornings, New Zealand tahr display a similar reluctance to begin grazing, as is reported in the Indian herds by Schaller. (In India the tahr wait until the sun is well up before commencing their limited winter journeys.) For this reason, on cold frosty mornings, there is little advantage to be gained by the winter hunter who is on the hunting grounds at first light.

During summer, however, the mid-day period of resting is shorter and the dawn and dusk feeding sessions are more prolonged. Also, feeding starts promptly at first light. Thus the summer hunter is often rewarded for making an early start, and able to spot animals as they move and feed. The spring and summer ranges of tahr mean the animals are at their lowest altitudes of the year, where matagouri and other scrub often grows. Spotting the animals in this scrub can be difficult. A knowledge of the vegetation preferences of tahr can, therefore, help you identify areas where time spent spotting is more likely to be fruitful.

Rumen studies

Studies of the rumen contents of tahr shot in the Rangitata/Rakaia area carried out by Dr J. Parkes in 1993 are summarised in Fig. 14. The results not only provide us with a season-by-season guide to the main items in the diet of tahr on the eastern alpine slopes, but also go some way to confirm the seasonal shifts in altitude mentioned earlier.

Bear in mind that on average silver tussock and its close relatives the *Poa* tussocks tend to occur at lower altitudes than the snow or *Chionocloa* tussocks. A study of fig. 14 will reveal that the winter diet of tahr consists of 40% snow tussocks, taken in the higher winter range of the animals. (In contrast, chamois eat very little snow tussock in winter.) Conversely, the consumption of snow tussocks by tahr falls in spring, to a minimum in summer as the herds shift to progressively lower altitudes. Likewise, as a consequence of this same downward movement, the consumption of silver and *Poa* tussocks rises to a maximum in spring and summer.

A further point of interest in the rumen studies is the year-round sustained and significant intake of dwarf broom and snowberry. This bears a striking similarity to the diet of chamois, and again exhibits seasonal variations, which are probably a consequence of both the ripening patterns of the plants and their physical availability. For example, in winter some plants may be inaccessible because they are covered in snow. Also, when a particular plant species is ripe to eat, it may not be at the altitude range where the tahr are currently feeding.

Thus, *Hebe* species are taken in the spring and summer, the giant buttercup in spring and Armstrong's speargrass in summer and autumn. Mountain daisies are consumed mostly in the winter and spring. In winter, along with the rising consumption of the *Chionocloa* tussocks, there is an increased intake of the lowly *Helicrysum*, dweller of the high rocky places.

Above: *This close-up of a chamois nanny shows the finer structure of the females' horns. Their length suggests a beast of a good few summers.*
Right: *A good chamois buck in summer coat. Note the elevated tail, a sign of alarm indicating that this animal has sensed all is not well.*
Below: *A typical view of a quarry, always watchful to hazard from below. Here, a chamois buck in darker winter coat casts a wary eye from a good vantage point.*

Left: *A young bull tahr pauses to warm itself in the early morning sun.*
Below: *A nanny with juvenile males photographed late in the rut. The mature nanny to the left is watching the juvenile bull give the lateral head-up display and show flehmen to another nanny out of the picture.*
Right: *A unique photograph of a mature bull tahr (third from left) giving a lateral head-up display from atop a rocky ridge.*

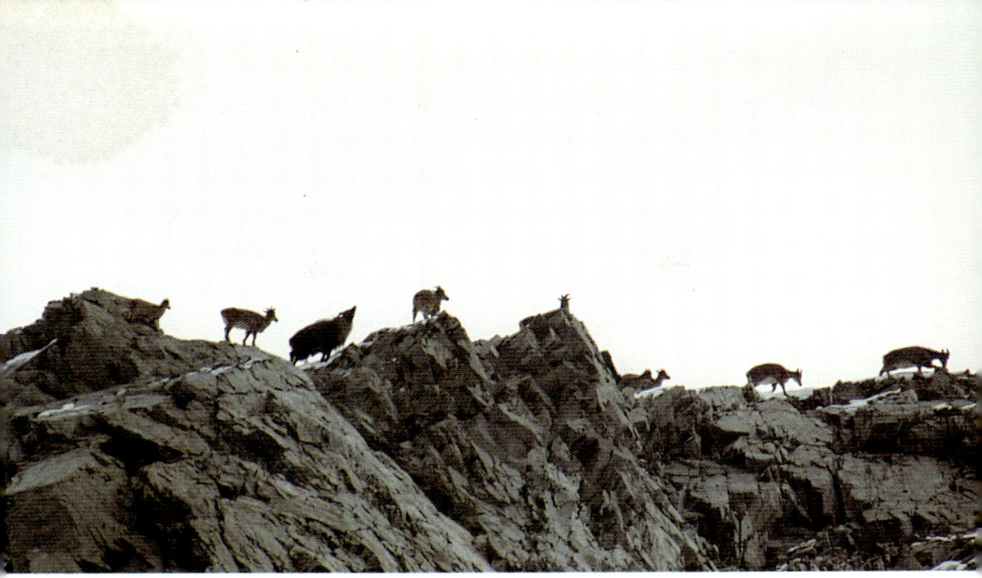

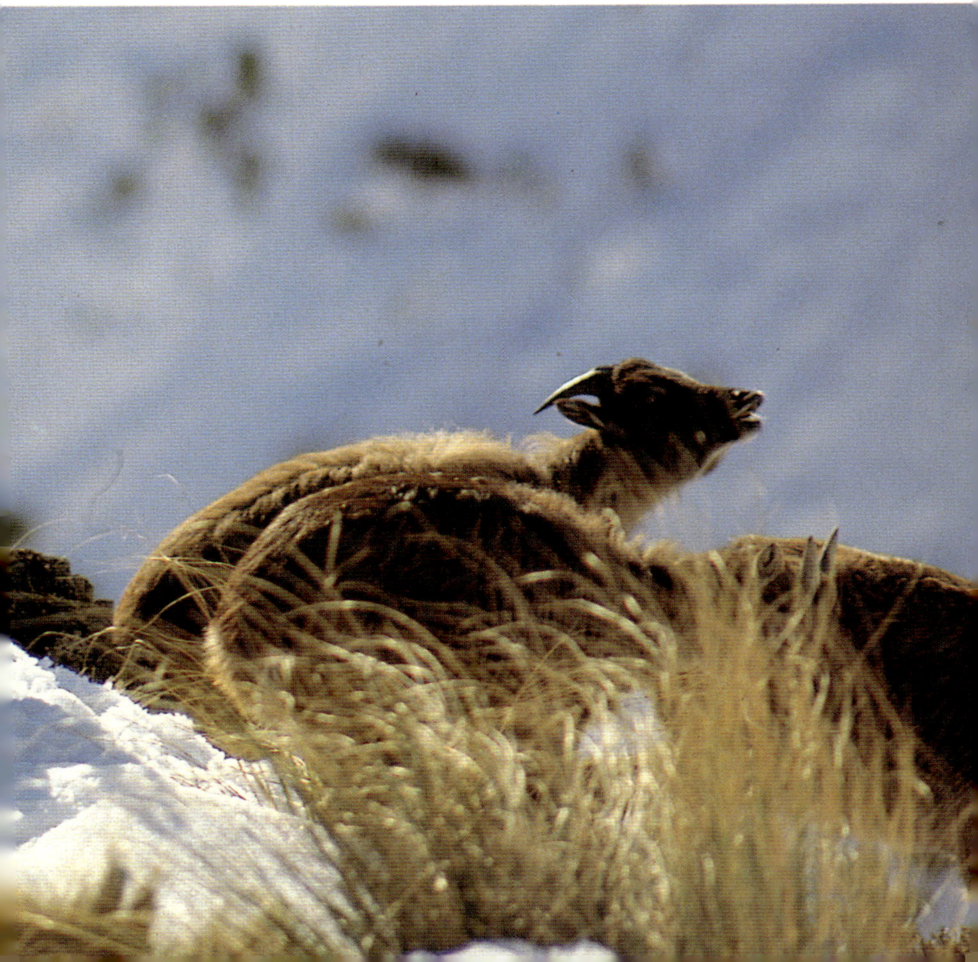

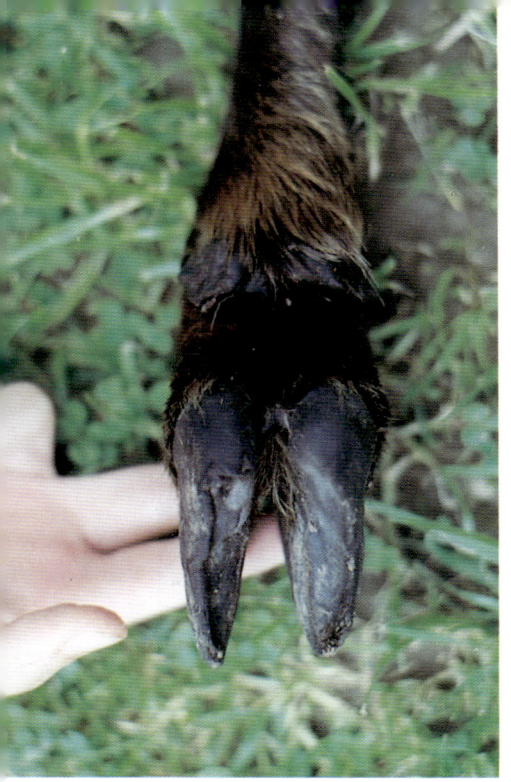

Top left: Hind foot of a buck chamois. Note the cleaves are only slightly longer than they are wide and that the dew claws are less developed than those of deer.
Above: Hind foot of a bull tahr. Again note the oblong appearance of the cleaves with the length nearly equal to the breadth. Of particular interest is the fact that the dew claws are barely visible, tucked in against the bulky dew pads. A further point of interest is the greater contrast between the horny rim of the cleaves and the inner pad. This is due to the greater softness of the inner pad compared to that of chamois. This is thought to allow better grip on rock.
Left: Hind foot of a red deer stag for comparison. The cleaves are longer and thinner and splay out more on soft ground. This structure is designed to sink in and grip in soft conditions whereas that of chamois and tahr holds together more, giving better traction on hard surfaces.

Hunting tahr

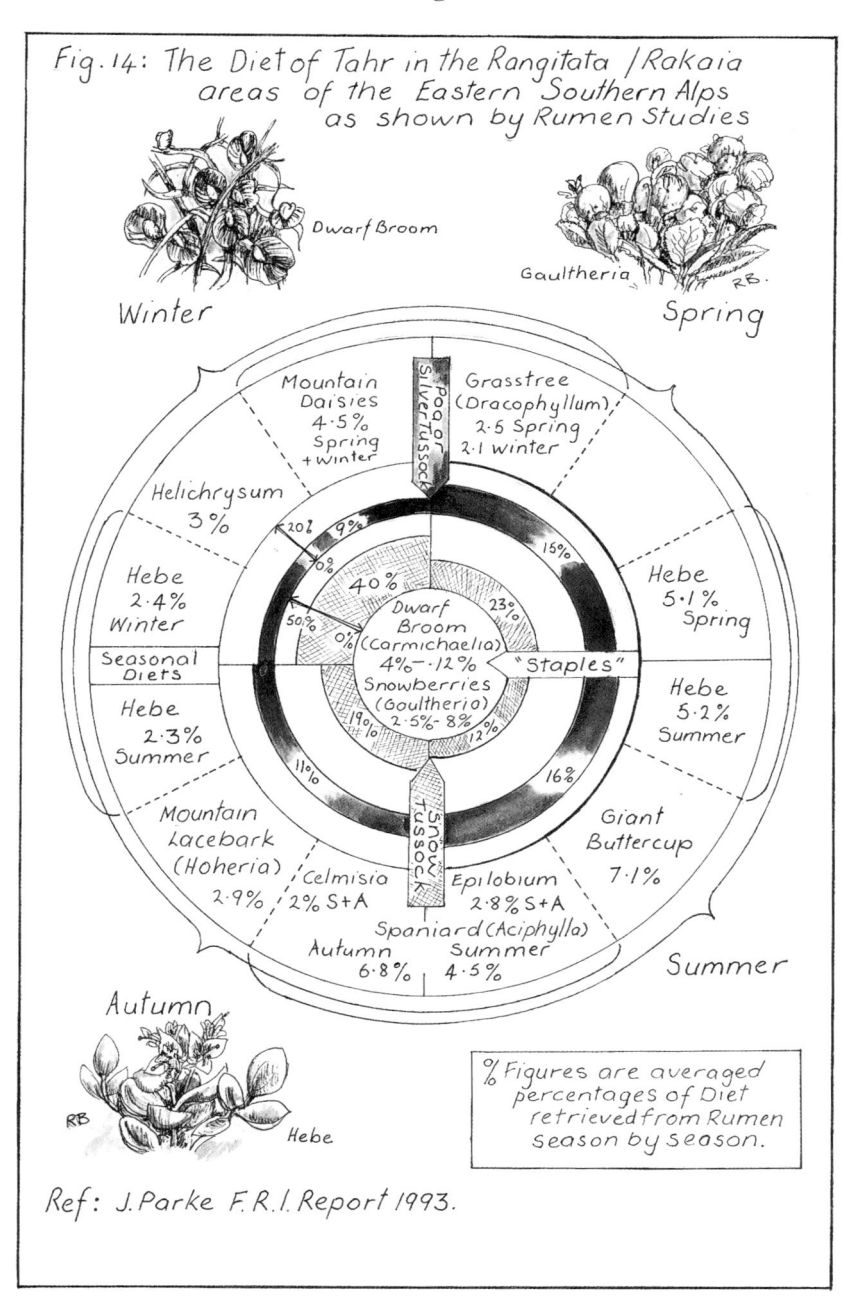

Fig. 14: The Diet of Tahr in the Rangitata/Rakaia areas of the Eastern Southern Alps as shown by Rumen Studies

Dwarf Broom

Gaultheria

Winter

Spring

Mountain Daisies 4.5% Spring + Winter

Grasstree (Dracophyllum) 2.5 Spring 2.1 Winter

Poa or Silver Tussock

Helichrysum 3%

Hebe 2.4% Winter

Hebe 5.1% Spring

Seasonal Diets

Dwarf Broom (Carmichaelia) 4% – 12%
Snowberries (Gaultheria) 2.5% – 8%

"Staples"

Hebe 5.2% Summer

Hebe 2.3% Summer

Mountain Lacebark (Hoheria) 2.9%

Celmisia 2% S+A

Snow Tussock

Epilobium 2.8% S+A

Giant Buttercup 7.1%

Spaniard (Aciphylla) Autumn 6.8% Summer 4.5%

Summer

Autumn

Hebe

% Figures are averaged percentages of Diet retrieved from Rumen season by season.

Ref: J. Parke F.R.I. Report 1993.

Vegetation zones and seasonal changes

Like chamois and goats, tahr seem to be able to eat almost anything that comes in their path. As they take their morning walk from low to higher altitude, they will therefore graze or browse more or less anything they encounter.

During the winter months tahr start their day, as we have seen, at a high altitude of around 1400 metres and feed on the plants they encounter at this height. In the Godley, this zone supports snow tussock and scrubby zones that contain snow totara and *Dracophyllum* species. A study in the Godley showed that during the months of June and July tahr spent roughly the same amount of time feeding in the tussock as they did in the scrub. They ate not only snow tussock, but also snow totara and *Dracophyllum* as they journeyed upwards. A good hunting strategy in this area would thus be to look for areas where there is clear separation of islands of scrub from surrounding snow tussock. Scan these areas and try to spot animals as they venture into the open tussock patches, especially during the morning and evening feeding periods.

In the spring, with the shedding of the thick insulating layer of underfur, tahr move to lower, warmer regions, camping up overnight at altitudes as low as 1000 metres. Starting from this height, the animals' usual dawn and dusk journeys will bring them now to encounter the same short *Poa* tussocks that their cousins the chamois prefer. Each morning, they spend longer feeding than in winter, eating *Poa* tussocks, as well as feeding in areas of matagouri, before climbing, feeding as they go, into the snow-tussock areas. By mixing a diet of fresh green shoots eaten at lower altitude early in the morning, and the old snow tussocks that are eaten later, the New Zealand tahr are selecting a diet comprising both new and old vegetation. It is interesting to note that in this respect it is similar to the diet that the tahr in Nepal also choose in spring.

If you are looking to find tahr feeding in spring, try first those areas of short tussock with islands of matagouri or other sub-alpine scrub. These will be located more down-slope and perhaps down-valley. Promptly at dawn you may see the animals emerge from the islands of scrub, where they are likely to have been bedded for the night. Your greatest chance of seeing them is while they are grazing the short tussock areas, where they are relatively easy to see. As the morning wears on they will gain altitude.

It may be, in fact, that part of the reason for the sudden and considerable spring descent of tahr is to intercept the spring growth at the lower altitudes. Circumstantial evidence for this comes from the fact that as summer wears on, the animals camp overnight at progressively higher altitudes. It seems that this matches the spring/summer tide of new growth as it ascends the mountainside. As summer advances, the hunter who is endeavouring to spot animals during their feeding times should concentrate his spotting efforts more up-slope and more up-valley. From January onwards, there is a steady monthly shift upwards of both bedding and feeding sites, so that by autumn the hunter will again find himself spotting the *Dracophyllum* and snow tussock areas.

One consequence of the change in the average height from which the animals start each day, is the fact that the height at which the mid-day rest is taken is also reduced. Thus, in spring and early summer the height at which the animals take their now short mid-day break is 1400 metres or thereabouts. This is the very height from which they start in winter. Thus the summer rest now puts the herds in the snow tussock and scrub areas at midday. Here they may be more easily reached with a cross-valley shot, but are much more difficult to spot. If you are working country where heavy cover at the bedding and morning shot levels makes for difficult spotting, you could consider waiting at the level of the summer mid-day rest. Here, with luck, you may encounter the animals coming up to you. This technique is often not feasible in the high frozen winter places, but is more practical on lower ground in the warmth of summer.

Tahr probably obtain all the moisture they need from the vegetation they eat. In any case, they have never been observed anywhere in the world to drink, nor to make journeys to and from water sources. Hence, even in the driest summer, plans to hunt stream beds so as to encounter tahr coming down for a drink are unlikely to be fruitful.

Social groups

Tahr are highly sociable — more so than chamois, for example. The most enduring social unit of tahr society, however, is the nanny/kid one-parent family. Groups of these one-parent families often come together and form herds of nannies and kids. Often they are joined by juvenile males as well. In this way, large groups of animals may form in undisturbed areas. Close observations in Nepalese herds have shown, however, that these herds do not have the tendency to stick together, nor do they have the degree of organisation that red deer groups do. Tahr groups tend to split into temporary sub-groups, and they may split up further. Sub-groups may then recombine with other groups in a random manner as the days and seasons change.

Some bulls associate with these female-dominated herds, or sub-groups. As we have seen, however, they are most often encountered only on the edge of them or some distance away — except during the rut. As the population builds up in an area, some of the males tend to leave the area altogether in a search for other pastures. Such males will most often be encountered as singletons; but sometimes, in a choice spot, numbers will build up to form bachelor groups or male herds. In some sites in New Zealand, it has been recorded that such bachelor groups will form in the summer, grazing new and distant pastures, only to return to their area of origin during the rut. Tustin and Challies, for example, reported that the head of Tom's Creek (a tributary of the Macauley) was populated only in summer, and by a herd consisting mainly of bulls. They presumed that these animals originally came from the adjacent, heavily populated Carneys Creek area, to which they returned during the rut and winter.

With regard to nannies and single-parent family groups, it is thought that these animals have a much greater tendency to stay put, and leave to colonize new areas only when conditions become really overcrowded.

Overall, Caughley found three basic units in tahr society:
1. The 'permanently resident' nanny/kid herds.
2. The temporary resident juvenile males.
3. The more permanently resident mature males.

These herd dynamics have important consequences for the hunter. The strong tendency for undisturbed nanny groups to stay in an area means that hunting the same ground where previously animals were numerous is very likely to pay off. This is doubly true when looking for a good trophy, as it is usually the younger males that leave an area. The dominant bulls are more likely to remain with or near the herd, while the intermediate bulls are likely to return to the fold, boosting numbers during the rut. On the other hand, particularly in areas where access difficulties exist, a good strategy is to scout adjacent watersheds for expatriate males of the type 2 unit.

Weather

It has been reported by New Zealand hunters that in times of bad weather, the animals will descend to lower altitudes to avoid it. In the light of what we have considered so far, such weather would need to be remarkably bad by deerstalking standards. Wind seems to have little effect on tahr; indeed it is sometimes, as we have seen, used as a cooling agent. Rain similarly has little effect on tahr in Nepal. Their cousins the Nilgiri tahr are reported to weather the monsoons with little obvious discomfort.

Snow cover is only of importance in two situations. Firstly, when heavy falls cover the feeding zone, we presume that the animals will be more or less forced to descend to maintain their food intake. Tahr, unlike their distant cousins the mountain sheep, have never been observed to 'paw' at snow cover in an effort to remove it. (But although their resting grounds higher up may be covered in snow, they are still easily able to use them.) Secondly, they seem to have an inbred fear of avalanche. Schaller reports tahr rapidly leaving areas upon the sound of rock-falls. Likewise, New Zealand hunters have noted from the studies of trails that the animals avoid potential avalanche fields of unstable snow. Thus the best time to encounter animals at a lower altitude is shortly after a heavy snowfall, when avalanche conditions prevail.

Hunting pressure

Effect on group size
It has been shown that heavy hunting pressure reduces the average size of tahr groups encountered. For example, a 93% reduction in animal numbers by intensive hunting reduced mean group size from 15.8 to 3.2 animals. Apart from showing the obvious, these figures show that even in the face of massive slaughter there continues to exist some cohesive force. Thus even in today's low animal densities you are still liable to encounter animals in groups. However, it also follows that when low densities of animals form groups, these are harder to find. More reason still to learn your quarry's habits.

Behaviour changes
Intensive shooting changes the behaviour of tahr. First there is overhang sheltering behaviour. Himalayan tahr initially tuck themselves in tightly against the rock wall at the base of cliffs at the first sound of

avalanche. This reaction has presumably evolved for protection against falling boulders. Both chamois and tahr also favour such places for bedding down at night, presumably for the same reasons. Helicopter shooters have found that tahr often take cover under overhangs, perhaps reacting to a noise that to them sounds like an avalanche. Although for the wrong reason, this behaviour is often effective, as hidden away under overhangs and in small caves in the mountains the tahr can be safe. Similarly, a distant rifle shot could be interpreted by the animals as an avalanche and cause the animals to seek shelter in a similar manner. In any case, it is a good strategy when hunting areas known to have been recently helicopter or ground-hunted to pay particular attention to such places.

Second, there is forest-sheltering behaviour. George Schaller, studying tahr in the eastern Himalayans, noted how tahr behaved when living alone and then what they did when two other species, the ibex and the bahral, came on the scene. These other two species are better adapted as grazers of the high pasture. He found that tahr would, as in New Zealand, spend a large part of their lives out in the mountain pastures when they had it to themselves. However, when the other species competed with them for the mountain pasture grazing, the tahr would often take up residence in the slightly lower altitude conifer/rhododendron forest. This shows how adaptable the species is, and in particular why in areas of high-altitude forest the animals may take up a forest-dwelling lifestyle when under great hunting pressure. To the hunter this means that a good hunting strategy in areas that are intensely hunted (particularly by helicopter) is to hunt the upper forest margins, especially in areas beneath extensive bluff systems.

With regard to the interaction of New Zealand tahr with other game animals, it seems that unlike the situation in the eastern Himalayas, our tahr have the upper hand over the alpine competition, chamois. Herds of tahr nannies always seem to displace chamois. Herds of bull tahr may sometimes be found living in the same area as chamois, but cause these chamois to switch their diet. (See p. 70 for a fuller explanation.)

Rutting

Nanny tahr have slightly longer pregnancies than female chamois (six-and-a-half as opposed to five-and-a-half to six months). Both species, however, naturally aim to give birth during spring, when maximum plant growth will aid milk production. However, there is a slight difference of timing because in New Zealand they are living in mountain conditions that are different to those in which they evolved. Tahr begin rutting in late May and are finished by late July. Chamois begin in early May, peaking in late May to early June, and are finished by mid-July. So although tahr theoretically should rut earlier than chamois to get the best spring conditions for the birth of their kids, they in fact rut later, their kids being born later in the spring than are chamois kids. (An alternative explanation for this 'mismatch' could be that tahr rut later because spring comes slightly later to the higher ground in which they live and thus their kids need to be born later.)

Rutting in both chamois and tahr is a somewhat low-key affair, with none of the more obvious trappings of the deer rut such as scrapes, wallows, rubbing posts or fraying stocks (although it is interesting to note that some of their near relatives, the mountain goats, dig rutting pits). Nevertheless, it is valuable to be able to correctly identify when the rut is on, as it can be a time of fruitful hunting. At this time, even the most wary bull tahr and chamois bucks have their minds on other things.

Scientists report increased movements of animals in the rut. In particular the male herds leave their summer pastures and return to the nanny/young territory. Increased movement means increased chance of sightings by hunters. With the return of the male groups, large mixed herds are formed. Within these herds it is thought each nanny holds a small territory and the males pay court to her. Caughley states that these small courting territories are approximately 1400 square metres in area.

The observation of mixed herds tells you the mating season is underway. However, to be really sure that mating is actually taking place, more careful observation is required. The flamboyant advertising behaviour of deer is replaced in both the tahr and chamois by more subtle signs. In tahr and chamois, males do not battle one another in claims to territory. The underlying theme is one of males displaying to what are judged to be receptive females and mating only once the consent of a female has been secured. There is little in the way of violent conflict: instead the same visual display that is given by males to the nannies often serves to intimidate lesser rivals.

In day-to-day life for both tahr and chamois scent sign is less important than visual cues. During the rut, however, the importance of

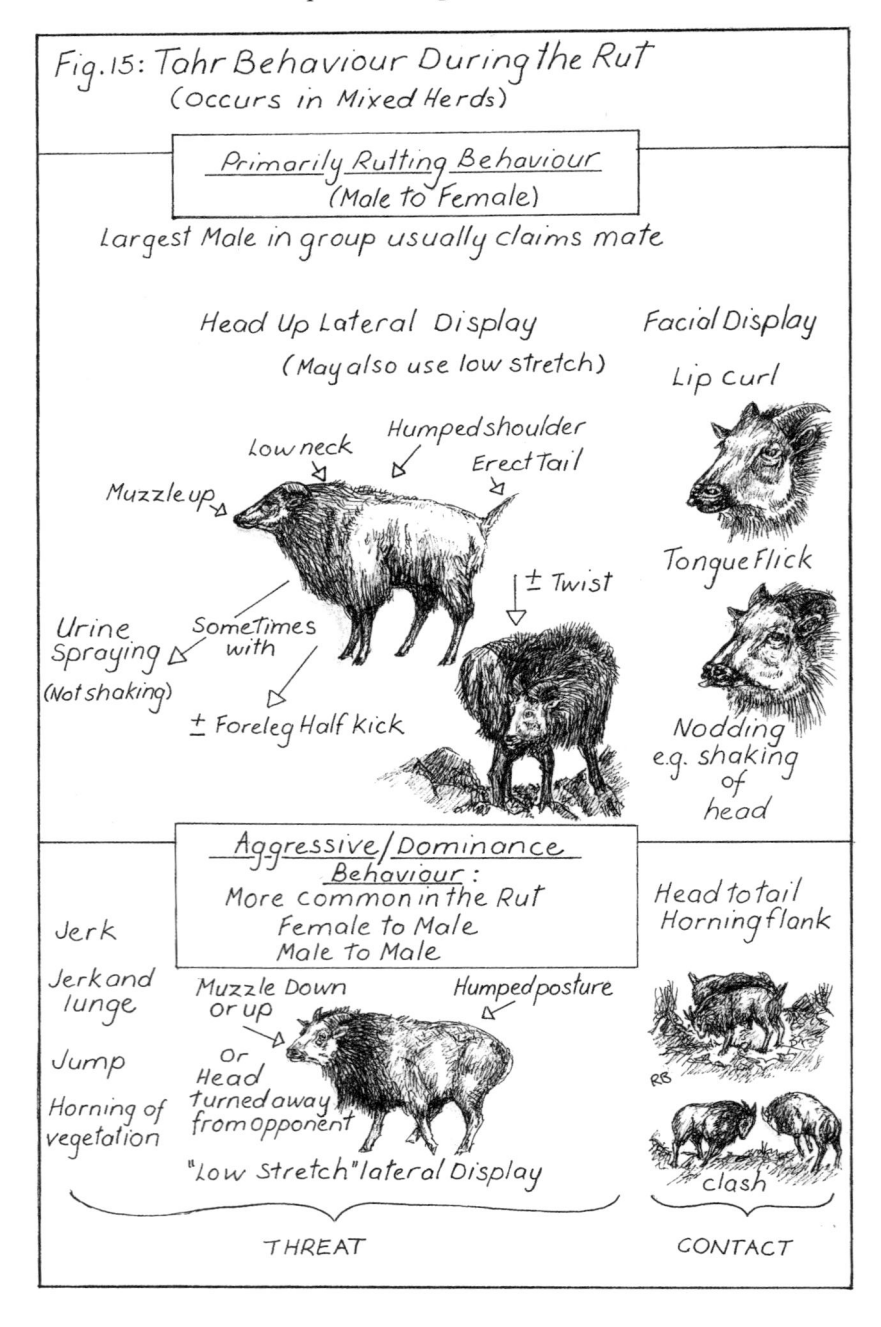

Fig.15: Tahr Behaviour During the Rut
(Occurs in Mixed Herds)

Primarily Rutting Behaviour
(Male to Female)

Largest Male in group usually claims mate

Head Up Lateral Display
(May also use low stretch)

- Muzzle up
- Low neck
- Humped shoulder
- Erect Tail
- ± Twist
- Urine Spraying (Not shaking)
- Sometimes with
- ± Foreleg Half kick

Facial Display
- Lip curl
- Tongue Flick
- Nodding e.g. shaking of head

Aggressive/Dominance Behaviour:
More common in the Rut
Female to Male
Male to Male

- Jerk
- Jerk and lunge
- Jump
- Horning of vegetation
- Muzzle Down or up
- Or Head turned away from opponent
- Humped posture
- "Low Stretch" lateral Display

THREAT

Head to tail Horning flank

clash

CONTACT

scent in chamois has been seen to greatly increase. In tahr, no such activities have been recorded. (Tahr, however, do possess some scent glands.) It may in fact be that at the higher and windier elevations inhabited by these animals scent cues are ineffective. Instead there is a marked reliance on visual body signals. The following signals have been noted (see also Fig. 15):

Lipcurl The bull curls his upper lip back, revealing his teeth. This display is typically seen when a bull sniffs a nanny's rear. It is probably akin to 'showing flehmen' in deer, whereupon the animal is able to detect a hormone in the nanny's urine that signals she is ready to mate. Although this behaviour is reported in New Zealand studies, Schaller says it is less common in tahr than chamois. He also says that chamois males tend to direct their displays at the rear end of nannies, whereas bull tahr direct their displays at the head end of their partners. This is probably another example of the fact that with tahr, the visual sense dominates.

Low-stretch This is the name given to the peculiar position adopted by a bull tahr when it approaches a nanny. The bull may low-stretch to the nanny's rear as a prelude to a lipcurl, or to her front as a seductive technique. In this display the head is lowered until the neck is almost parallel to the ground. The animal's muzzle is drawn back and pointed upward (See the photographs in the colour section.) The drawing back action accentuates the hump of the shoulder muscles at the same time as displaying the erected hairs of the prominent ruff. On top of this basic low-stretch display pattern, the following behaviours may be added:

Head-shaking The head is suddenly jerked downwards in a swift nod while at the same time being shaken tremulously from side to side.

Kicking During the head-shake display, a half-hearted kick of the foreleg that does not ever strike the nanny.

Tongue flicking The tongue is flicked rapidly in and out of the mouth in a similar action to that sometimes seen in red stags 'showing flehmen'.

Twisting During the low-stretch approach to a nanny, a bull may sometimes hold his head at an angle to his neck with his horns pointing away from the nanny.

The side-on silhouette of the bull in the low-stretch position seems to be the most potent image used to secure female consent, and displaying males thus strive to position themselves so this occurs.

Similarly, the side-on profile seems effective at dissuading lesser bulls. Two competing males have at times been observed standing parallel to one another, head to tail, displaying in this manner.

All observers have commented on the comparative gentleness of rutting behaviour. That is not to say that body contact does not happen. Indeed, it seems principally to occur when a younger bull is rebuffed by a nanny. This contact is most commonly a butt delivered by the nanny to the shoulders or retreating rump of a courting male. On other occasions it seems that the mere threat of contact is sufficient, especially when the nanny is pestered by a juvenile male. Such threats by nannies can take the form of a jump forward 'at the rear', a jerk of the head with horn toward the opponent, or a lunge with the head in a similar position. Clashing of heads does not seem to occur as an act of female repulsion. It has, however, been reported, rarely, between bulls. It has also been seen between yearling males and females, probably as an act of play.

Thus the rut continues to its conclusion, with body contact rare. To give you an idea of an actual mating we reproduce here an account of one observed in the Himalayas. In these next two descriptions, the males have been classified into three classes. Class I (3 years or less), class II (4-5 years) and class III (5+ years).

> At 0815, a female is attended by a class III male and two class II males, all somewhat separated from the main group. When a class II male approaches the female, the class III male by her side advances toward him in a hunch display (humped approach). The smaller male turns aside, joins the other class II male, and both rest at least 10 metres from the courting pair. The class III male assumes the low-stretch, but the female ignores it and he reclines.
>
> At 0910 hours the approach of a class II male brings him to his feet, and a hunch display causes the interloper to veer off. Once again he faces the female in a low-stretch. For 15 minutes they stand, he with muzzle raised, she with head averted. After that both feed and rest.
>
> At 1105 hours, the female approaches the male who lifts his muzzle so high that the underside of the jaw faces her. She licks herself, advances, licks again. Whenever she moves, he adjusts his position so that his muzzle points at her. Suddenly he steps behind her, his shoulder by her rump. He gives a low-stretch coupled with a twist, then shakes his head and kicks. Twice more he shakes and kicks before moving around to face the motionless female. There he alternatively low-stretches with teeth bared and shakes a total of nine

times. Occasionally he nudges the female with his nose as if to get her attention, for when she looks at him he intensifies his low-stretch.

The female begins to feed at 1200 hours. Slowly the male steps behind her and rears on his hindlegs, mounting her. He thrusts ten times, barely leaning against her, without eliciting a response. The two then feed and rest near each other without further courting for several hours (Schaller, 1973a.)

In this following example of an unsuccessful approach of a male to a female, we can see why many big-game workers believe than in these species the male is socially inferior to the female.

A group of sixteen tahr is scattered over a cliff. At 1050 hours a class II male approaches a female and gives the low-stretch in front of her. He stands with muzzle raised and head turned to one side for five minutes before he shifts his gaze to face her directly. She has her neck lowered and muzzle pointed downward. Soon he assumes a similar posture. (Both the averted glance and lowered head seem to be gestures of submission, showing lack of aggressive intent). After a few minutes the female suddenly jabs him lightly in the neck, but he merely lowers his head still more. Both stand motionless. When the male raises his head, she jabs him again, and he promptly assumes his former position.

One hour after meeting the female, the male gives an intensive low-stretch, muzzle straining skyward, then turns aside, licks himself, and ambles off. A class III male has been lying in full view 30 metres away. He now displays the low-stretch to the female, grazes by her side a few minutes, then drifts off too. (Schaller 1973.)

Spotting herds

Here are a few more hints on spotting tahr.

Ridges
A characteristic of tahr behaviour (particularly the bulls in winter coat) is that they will stand for long periods on the edge of high ridges, allowing strong winds to buffet them. So, if you are trophy hunting, make a good search of ridges and spurs. The habit of standing on a ridge is often undertaken by one or two animals belonging to a bigger group settled at their high mid-day altitude resting position. Thus, late morning to early afternoon is a good time for spotting tahr this way.

Tahr standing on ridges are often relatively easy to spot. When viewed from below, their neck and head often stand out above the ridge line, sometimes silhouetted against the sky. The waving movement of a tahr's neck-mane often gives it away, especially when viewed thorough a pair of binoculars. Sometimes animals a very long way above can be spotted in this way. Unfortunately, spotting the animals high above is often the easier part of the problem. They may be so high and inaccessible, especially in winter, that getting up there is beyond you.

Sunny spots
Tahr actively seek out a sunlit spot to lie in, particularly during the middle part of the day when they rest and cud. In winter the beasts are often above the vegetation line and with a bit of patient spotting can be found bedded in rocky basins or even on snow.

Other factors
The effect of season and vegetation are complex but important. See pages 85, 90 and 93.

When to look
Tahr are easier to spot when on the move. If you closely observe areas known to hold tahr during the period of morning and evening feeding, when the animals are moving most, you will often find them. In some cases this will involve watching areas that contain scrub or *Dracophyllum*. In amongst this taller vegetation tahr are more difficult to keep under observation. Nevertheless, spotting animals under these conditions is still reputed to be easier than when they are relatively still and crouched on open ground. Apart from ease of spotting, if you find beasts at lower altitude in feeding areas they will be easier to reach and the shooting will be at shorter range. This is because the animals are lower down in the V of the valley cross-section so the distance across from hunter to target is correspondingly shorter.

If you don't find animals eating and on the move in among the vegetation by late morning, you should systematically and minutely search the ground, looking for resting animals higher up. Remember the height of these resting places varies with the season, tending to be higher in winter than in summer, for example.

What to do after spotting tahr
Having spotted a herd, say on the opposite side of a valley, you face a

choice of hunting strategies. You can take a very long shot — sometimes with the range reduced by climbing upwards on the opposite side to a point immediately across from the animals. Or, if you have the nerve, you can cross the valley and stalk up to them in true mountaineering style. Alternatively, you can choose a lower spot immediately below the herd's current position. There the two sides of the valley are likely to have come closer together and thus reduced the distance across. There you can wait in ambush until the evening feeding descent of the herd brings them within range (hopefully).

Eastern versus western hunting in the alps

Experienced tahr hunters will have noticed in the previous section that much material refers to hunting in the southern alps. There are, of course, currently populations of tahr to the east of the main southern alps, for example in the Two Thumbs Range. The future of the eastern herds is currently in the balance following a ministerial report on the future of the tahr. For this reason we have not devoted much space to techniques specific to hunting the eastern herds.

Broadly, the techniques of hunting herds east of the main divide are the same as in the west. However, the further east one goes, the less forest cover there is. Provided your spotting techniques are sound, this lack of forest cover allows for easier hunting. Dietary habits also show slight differences between east and west. In the east the animals have to rely mainly on tussock, and while there is little scientific data on grass preferences and seasonal shifts, it seems the eastern animals are much more mobile and less likely to follow particular seasonal ripening patterns through altitude changes. The location of animals using a knowledge of feeding characteristics is thus much less of a science. A more hit-and-miss hunting approach is usually adopted.

In the Two Thumbs Range, particularly, the country is less steep. This makes for fewer areas of potential snow-slip, providing high altitude grazing sites in winter. Without these, the animals are forced into a more general pattern of retreat to lower ground when there is a heavy snow cover, and thus do not exhibit the same degree of upward migration with winter coat. To the hunter, this means reverting to the old-style deerstalking trick of picking out wintering-over areas at lower altitude where there is less snow cover and where winter grazing is available.

Trophy potential

Tahr (and chamois) do not shed their horns as deer do. Instead they add extra growth at the base of their horns each year. This forms an annual horn ring. This ring is laid down when the animal has a good food intake: in spring, summer and autumn. In winter, when food intake is lower, additions to the year's growth almost cease and thus a break appears in the ring. In this manner, year by year, horn rings separated by breaks build up below one another as the horn grows longer. The animal's age can be worked out by counting the rings. In New Zealand tahr the growth rings are readily distinguishable — unlike those of chamois.

When considering any game animal group's trophy potential there are three factors to consider. These are the age structure of the group, their genetics and their nutrition. We shall now consider these factors with respect to tahr.

The age structure of the group
In areas where there is little in the way of hunting pressure, more animals will live longer. This enables more rings to be added by the older members of the group, and so longer horns result.

Genetics
The amount of horn laid down each year is to some extent influenced by the genetic programme of the beast. All animals start by adding large segments in their early years but as they get older the amount added each year gets less. However, in some animals this decrease is less pronounced than others. Year for year, these beasts add more length of horn compared to the average animal. This trait is in their genetic make-up.

If you are a dedicated tahr (or chamois) trophy hunter you would therefore benefit from keeping careful records of the location of animals shot, together with the length of their annual horn additions. This information is valuable even if no trophy-length horns are taken. From this data, you may be able to identify strains of beasts that grow a greater than average annual length. You can then focus on the area where this strain lives and hopefully obtain a head from an older animal. By virtue of its greater than average annual horn increments, this beast is likely to be of top trophy class. (See Appendix 1.)

Nutrition

In areas where there are high densities of animals there is more likely to be a shortage of the food (most notably proteins) required for good horn growth. Animals that live in high-density areas are likely to have less annual horn additions than average. Areas where there are lower animal densities and good year-round food supply are therefore more likely to yield top trophies. Under modern conditions this 'over-population' problem is less of a consideration as intensive shooting, in particular by helicopter, has typically reduced animal densities well below carrying capacity.

Nevertheless, the social habits of tahr may sometimes create local food shortage areas. In particular, undisturbed tahr have a tendency to build up large numbers but remain in small territories. This diminishes the amount of food available locally.

Plant growth, however, varies with good and bad years, and this introduces another variation to the annual growth-rings of horn. (These annual fluctuations make studies of the kind described in the genetics section above more difficult to interpret.)

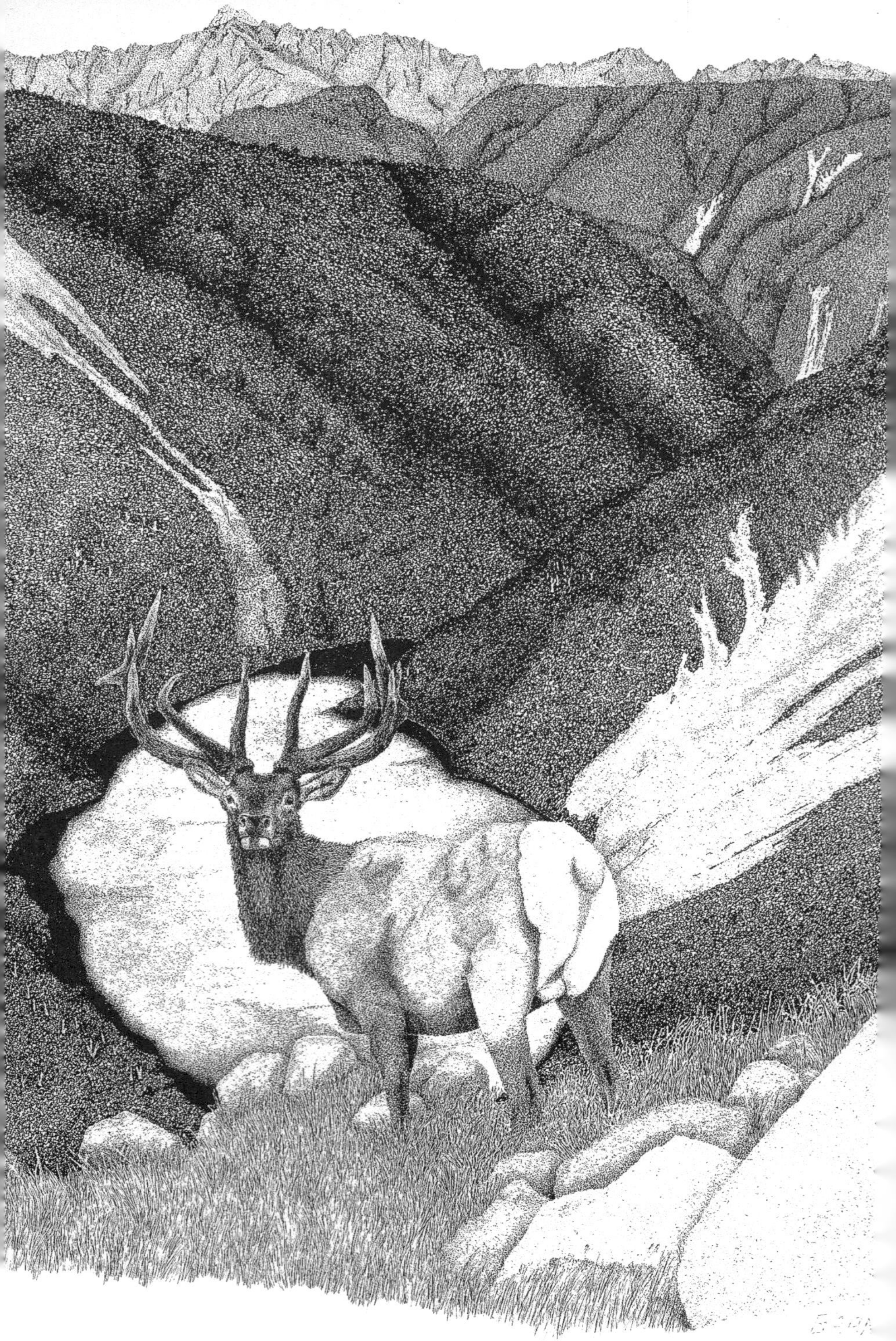

Deer

> Nowhere have I felt more the ephemeral nature of individual man than after spending some days alone in this grey and broken country.
>
> F. Frazer Darling, *A Herd of Red Deer*

5
Deer in the mountains

Fiordland is a dramatic land. Nothing there is done in half-measures.

I went there for the bugle of 1992. While others remained in their hangars, our helicopter pilot pulled his chopper out, and dodging low cloud and severe rain squalls flew us the long way round to land us on our block on the sea coast at Two Thumb Bay. For the first seven days, the weather forecast on the mountain radio each night predicted either a gale or a severe gale. There were spectacular showers of hail, where the white frozen rain flew sideways in huge sheets across the sea and the estuary below our base camp.

Between these fast and furious cold fronts, brief clearer weather presented itself and we hunted the river valley. We even carried a fly-camp up-valley for five hours and spent three days hunting the bush in between storms. On one of these days, Warren Plum and I went high on a ridge. However, it was covered in short, tight vegetation and there was no animal sign. The weather didn't allow us to explore higher. The day we walked back down-valley to base, the weather began to clear. By that time seven days had passed and we had seen sixteen deer in total. With the exception of a young bull, the animals we encountered at lower altitude were more red than wapiti in characteristic. The weather had frustrated our plans to hunt high in the alpine regions of our block.

But when at last it's fine in Fiordland, it seems to me there is no better weather anywhere in the world. The next day was a fine day, a day clean and bright, a day my father would describe as 'one out of the box'.

From the coast of Two Thumb Bay up to the high dividing ridge system between it and Looking Glass Bay is a good steady pull of three hours. Shortly after daybreak on this fine day in late March, Eric Hall and I set off to climb it. I went in front, as it was my turn to shoot; I hadn't fired a shot on this trip so far. Eric had bagged two stags and

Deer in the mountains

Warren had shot a good 10-point animal just the day before. It carried wapiti characteristics in its antler formation, although its body colour and size was more red deer-like. The antlers scored about 254 on the Douglas score. Last night we had celebrated this event with a bottle of whisky; I had drunk too much, and was feeling its effects this morning.

We struggled up through tight kiekie on steep terrain to capture the first 200 metres of elevation. Once above this level, and the influence of salt spray, we found easier travelling on a bush spur, and we found sign. A wallow recently used — probably that night. We searched for clues to which way he had gone, but we didn't find a lot and we didn't linger. We wanted to travel a long way on this day. In any case, his prints were not huge. Furthermore, the understorey here was thick crown fern, not easy to follow trail in. Higher up it would be clearer and better for reading sign.

Spurs lead to ridges, which climb up to other ridges and finally to the top of a hill. All that a hunter needs to do is to persist upwards. Three hours after leaving camp, we arrived on a high point of the major ridge. In a long curve it puts an arm above Looking Glass Bay to lead to some distant, unnamed tops. We took a break and sat in a place where the sunlight penetrated the canopy, falling onto the forest floor, and ate some food. For the first time in eight days my hunting clothes were beginning to dry out!

Here on the ridge-top the forest understorey was open. I could see up to 100 metres ahead in places. Pepperwoods now replaced crown fern and the ground was easier to find and read deer sign in. A benefit of the storms in this land is that they clear the ground of deer sign; hence any footprints found are new.

We carried on. No response, wapiti or red deer, to our imitation red-deer roaring — unfortunately. As we climbed higher, the route along the top of the ridge became clearer. Also the understorey became dominated by areas of tall leatherwoods. We marvelled at the sign of where the animals had broken off leatherwood branches to keep the way clear. It was wide enough for a trophy set of antlers to pass, and, open enough underneath to form summer thermal cover.

What a tremendous feeling to be up high in wapiti country, walking their routes, knowing nobody else had done so for at least three to five years if our pre-trip information-gathering was correct. Not far ahead we could expect to find the bush giving way to areas of tussock. Ideal country for rutting stags with wapiti genes to take up occupancy!

Two sections of the route held fresh prints, but the animals must have been down off the side, as we saw none. Nor did we have any response to Eric's occasional roar through a plastic tube. Then, clear in the dark soil of a soft section of route, we found some more fresh sign, including a huge set of bull prints. The forest was marvellously open at this point, with only scattered leatherwood. I felt my mate Eric hanging back. He was maybe 40 metres behind, leaving me clearly in the lead. He sensed a chance was about to present itself. I looked and looked ahead of me and to the sides as I walked. I seldom took time to look down at the ground. As well, I was listening intently in the clear air.

Then, there was something: the tops of two legs leading to a neck supporting a big set of antlers. A wapiti bull looked directly at me from 75 metres. Slowly raising my rifle I scrutinised him through the scope. I would need to move to get a rest, and it could easily disturb him. Holding my rife ever so carefully I squeezed the trigger. The animal collapsed at the shot. On running up to him, I realised how huge he was in body size. He was by far the biggest-bodied stag I had ever shot — and the one with the biggest antlers. There are probably no more pure wapiti left in Fiordland. The best are like this boy — close to being pure.

After helping take photos and remove the headskin, Eric left for an hour to stalk further along the ridge. Meanwhile I took the headskin off the skull and cut off the jaw.

About five minutes along the ridge, Eric found a small isolated tussock knoll. Here he walked onto a couple of hinds and a spiker. They must have been my bull's harem. He presumably had left them there and travelled down the ridge to investigate an intruder with the roar of a red stag (us).

Eric arrived back just as I finished my work. It was time to head for home. The main ridge we were on rises above short streams flowing down to the sea below. It is easy to follow along, but to get from it to camp below is the problem. To attempt to retrace our steps would be difficult. It would be easy to get the navigation wrong and come out onto sea bluffs too far north. We chose a less risky new route and travelled to the very end of the ridge before heading down into the main valley.

We started off with me carrying the antlers and headskin, and Eric the two rifles. When we finally made camp, tired, Eric was carrying the antlers. To get back we had spent two exhausting hours crabbing sideways on bluffs — we still didn't get it right. Damn that glacial-wall country between the valley floor and the alpine tops above. It is the bane of the alpine hunter in Fiordland.

In the lamp-light, back at camp, Warren measured the Douglas score of my head at 266, with a length of about 40 inches. **FS**

No discussion of alpine hunting in New Zealand would be complete without reference to deer. We have in our previous two books discussed in detail the more lowland dwelling places of deer and so will not repeat material here. Instead, we will concentrate on describing those situations where deer may be encountered by an alpine hunter.

Problems of deer living at high altitude

In *Stalking the Seasons Round* we discussed the advantage that large-bodied deer such as wapiti have in colder high-altitude conditions. This is due to the lower surface area to body size ratio of larger beasts, which results, in turn, in a smaller loss of body heat in cold situations. This increased cold tolerance enables these deer to exploit food sources that are available in colder upland regions. A larger body size, however, also means that these deer will have difficulty in getting rid of excess heat in warmer conditions. It has been shown that wapiti, while able to tolerate the frigid high tops in winter, need to seek shelter from the sun on warm sunny days.

There are advantages and disadvantages to being larger-bodied, and deer which have evolved this feature to exploit the higher alpine slopes are forced to lead a specialized lifestyle. If you understand the mechanisms involved, you will be better able to pick the conditions when you are likely to encounter deer on the high pastures.

Let us consider wapiti. The impressive body size of this species is thought to have evolved not only as a protection against cold but also to enable these deer to carry extensive fat stores. This need arose, again, from the alpine conditions in which they lived. During the summer months the grasslands on which the beasts feed are highly productive, giving a plentiful source of protein and carbohydrate — admittedly with a high fibre content. In winter, on the other hand, these same slopes are mostly covered in deep snow. The alpine life, therefore, means abundant food in the warmer months and a shortage in the colder ones. The animals need to feed up in the summer and carry a large store into the winter.

Individual species

Wapiti
When not harassed by helicopters, wapiti can be found feeding intensively on the tussock lands during spring and summer — particularly

on cooler days. On hotter days they may, for reasons we have already discussed, be forced to retreat to 'summer thermal cover' (see *Stalking the Seasons Round*, pp. 92-94). Again, because of their bulk and ability to tolerate more fibrous food, wapiti bulls will, at least in theory, be found higher and living on coarser grasses than the cows. So important is it for these beasts to maintain an intake of the best possible fodder, that they will follow the spring 'wave' of grass ripening. They will move upwards following this 'wave' as the spring develops into summer. As well, they will follow it around the valley sides, from the north-facing slopes which ripen first, onto the colder, later-ripening, south-facing ones.

Like other deer, wapiti move most at dawn and dusk. Noon on a hot summer day, for example, is liable to find them sheltering in breezy spots. On the short winter days when they are feeding, they do so most at dawn and dusk, with a consequently shorter daytime rest. However, overall they feed much less in winter, for the reasons we have already discussed. Total food intake may drop to a third in red deer, and as low as a tenth in larger, cold-climate deer.

The wapiti rut or bugle, in March/April, is likely to be a productive time for the alpine hunter. Wapiti bulls have a habit of selecting rutting grounds in the upper bush edges. They particularly favour places where small bush stands are separated by areas of tussock. From these vantage points, their high-pitched calls (somewhat similar to a yodel) enable the alpine hunter to zero in on the prey.

Although the wapiti rut is early compared to that of red deer, winter has usually started in those higher places that wapiti bulls frequent, so there is little in the way of a post-rut feeding spell and the hunter will therefore see an abrupt downturn in the hunting prospects by the finish of the mating season.

Hybrids and hunting pressure Everything that we have said so far applies to pure-bred wapiti living in conditions of minimal hunting pressure. However, in New Zealand these conditions rarely exist. Firstly, there has been extensive helicopter hunting of the open tops and thus the animals have become more cautious, some even spending most of their life under cover. However, the animals' basic needs continue, and any relaxation of pressure results nowadays in a more guarded (often nocturnal) emergence onto the tussocks, particularly during the great hunger of summer.

Secondly, there has been such extensive hybridization between red deer and wapiti that a whole range of variants is said to exist between the two pure breeds. In red deer the need for grass is not as strong, the animals being quite able to exist on bush tucker. Again, the summer hunger of reds is not so great as that of wapiti: red stags and hinds both feed intensively after the roar. Thus hybrids can be expected not to favour tussock feeding, particularly if they are subject to hunting pressure. With an increasing red-deer gene content in the Fiordland herds, the sometimes reckless summer behaviour of wapiti on the tops is likely to be replaced by the more cautious approach of the new hybrid animals.

On the other hand, red deer stags are known to have a greater ability to deal with high dietary fibre than red hinds. For this reason they are able to live in higher areas than their female counterparts. Injection of some wapiti blood into red stags sometimes results in an enhanced ability of the red stag hybrids to digest high-fibre food. Thus in areas of low hunting pressure, there is a greater likelihood of these animals emerging onto the tussock edges to feed.

Red deer

As every experienced hunter knows, red deer often emerge on to the tussock tops to feed. This is particularly so when there are high numbers of animals living in the bush. The alpine hunter is liable to encounter these animals feeding at the tussock edges, particularly during the summer months. Stags in particular show this tendency.

Stags have another problem in spring and summer that is solved when they move out of the bush. The velvet covering over the developing antler is particularly sensitive before it hardens. The more open conditions of the tussock therefore appeal. Thus you should pay particular attention to the tussock edges in late spring and summer.

Other times when red deer are particularly likely to emerge from the upper bush edges are:

In early spring With the first spring thaw, the snow mats begin to melt and expose a natural silage of compressed grasses. This acts as a magnet to hungry deer, particularly after a bad winter and in areas where bush-browse is poor.

After sudden heavy snow The weight of thick snow can cause broadleaf and other palatable shrubs in the subalpine zone to snap off. Stags particularly will move up in the bush to feed on these broken branches. Sometimes they will emerge from the bush to travel from one area of such browse to another.

The roar Early in the roar, stags often use the high tops as a route for travelling to the rutting area. During the roar proper, a travelling stag will often work along the bush edge at dawn and dusk, listening to the stags below him roaring. From the roars, he tries to pick a stag of his own size or smaller in order to mount a challenge. Also, a stag that is ensconced with territory and wallow will sometimes emerge from the bush into a tussock basin to use it as a resonator for his evening or morning roar. In today's era of helicopter hunting, it is rare for stags to wallow or hold hinds in the tussock fields themselves. If you are going to be on the tops during the rut, it is important to be in position above the tussock edge well before first light for a morning shot. Also, on an evening shoot stay there until the very last of the light. The changes from day to night and vice versa are particularly active times for rutting stags.

Set to the east of the main divide lies a much-folded wedge of land that still harbours a population of the alpine hunter's quarry. Sandwiched between the great braided river catchments of the Godley and the Rangitata, it is inextricably linked to the main range of the Southern Alps. Because of this simple geographic factor, even though from time to time it is hunted by helicopter gunships, the area is readily repopulated by migratory chamois and the occasional group of tahr Here and there, in scrubby gullies and clefts among rock-walled buttresses that offer cover from prying gunships, the hunter's crunching step can still draw an occasional shrill whistle of alarm.

The main problem for hunters is access, for in this region there are extensive leaseholds and the hunting is available only 'by grace and favour'. However, persistence is worthwhile, especially in late autumn when the first layers of the winter snow pack yield enough white rime to reveal tell-tale animal tracks, yet not enough to impede the hunter. Hence, in this season of the waning grass, I can still be found on occasion on the fringes of the Mackenzie Country.

One particularly gratifying trip was to the Ben Mcleod area. On that crisp autumn morning, perplexed residents of Sherwood Downs looked out to see what might have appeared to be a group of skiers heading up the Foxes Peak track to a field of grossly insufficient snow. The more knowledgeable runholders, however, were not fooled: their permission had already been secured, though they would perhaps have felt a moment's envy as the little LJ50 buzzed past in the early glow of dawn.

As the road swung west into the beginnings of the North Ophia river valley we could just discern a distant glint on the skyline where the snow was thick enough to gather a reflection from the rising eastern glow. Three hours later, with the Suzuki parked and a long climb behind us, we trod the same thin white crust and paused to glass into the headwaters of the river. We were still 1000 metres below the summit of Foxes Peak, and had scant regard for its morning grandeur, preoccupied as we were with the intricacies of spotting. From where we sat on the northern aspect of the peak, the three main tributaries of the Ophia could be viewed in detail as they cascaded downwards. About us was still an undulant sea of tussock, inundated but not yet submerged by the advancing tide of snow. On the higher ground there was a more uniform cover of white blanketing scree and fellfield alike. The only breaks in the white monotony were coal-black patches that signified small tarns, discernible in the headwaters of each stream.

At last, after half an hour's careful scrutiny, just as the shivers of inactivity had spread up our backs to a degree that made holding steady difficult, we spotted a distant tracery of track sign. It was only just discernible, being on the upper limit of the farthest of the three creeks, in an area known as the Butler Saddle. To reach it would probably take a whole day's traversing and certainly mean a long walk back across the flats to the ski road in the dark, but we were all game to try.

We started out well, stomping our way across the shoulder toward the first creek and crossing each of the creek's little tributaries with ease. By ten o'clock we had breasted out onto the shoulder between the first and second creeks, and paused to catch our breath and scan the ground ahead. The sign on the Butler Saddle, closer now, was re-evaluated and confirmed as animal track. We plodded onward through the shallow snows of the second basin, thinking only of our goal. Then a whistle stopped us dead. We all promptly sat down, rifles propped up, gazing about us, each keeping still yet searching desperately to spot the animal. The whistle was repeated, more distant now. Again the desperate search. I had just given up on the limited field of view afforded by my telescopic sight and switched to binoculars, when the source of the disturbance made his appearance. A buck chamois had been feeding in the creek, below our line of traverse, and must have plunged downward into the second creek as soon as he saw or heard us. Then, there he was, running headlong around the ridge that formed the opposite side of the creek.

Just as I dropped my binoculars to regain the grip on my rifle, the animal reached the crest of the ridge and paused for a moment, looking back. An explosion to my left told that one of my mates had hazarded the snap 200-metre shot. I listened intently but was not able to hear the sound of a bullet strike before a booming ripple of echoes came back at us from the surrounding peaks. The sound seemed to go on and on, rolling backwards and forwards like thunder, a warning to every other beast for miles.

Barely had the sound died when each member of the party, released from the awe of it, took his own independent course, racing to cross the creek and crest the ridge the chamois had just left, hoping to find either a downed animal or at least catch another glimpse of him. Always the last sprinter in a group of fit back-country farmers, I trailed the others and was last to join a pretty disconsolate pair. By the time I arrived the buck was nowhere to be seen, either dead or alive. His trail dropped neatly away into the lower, darker recesses of the last gully and bore not a trace of blood. A debate was raging as to whether the maker of the sign on the Butler saddle would have heard the shot. My own opinion was that it couldn't have failed to, for the final creek was now just ahead. (Indeed, the racket created by the .30/06 had so reverberated that I considered the wild possibility that even the residents of Fairlie had heard it!)

Dejectedly, we were considering whether to start our homeward journey by descending the spur on which we were sitting, when the final player of that memorable day made his appearance as a dark shape moving purposefully downwards on the opposite side of the final creek into which we now gazed. Obviously he had heard and been disturbed by the single shot, but had been unable to pinpoint the source. Now he was moving down into cover from the Butler Saddle area where we had spotted his tracks, to the safe haven of the tighter gully below. Obviously he had not seen us, for his course would bring him directly opposite us on the other face of the final gully.

As he moved downward, the snow flying from his feet barely 130 metres distant, three rifles spoke as one and the beast was killed instantly. Not a chamois, but a takeable red stag. In spite of the slightly shorter way back, it was still fully dark before we reached the little rag-top. Nevertheless we were happy with our burdens of rack and meat — each of us sure that his had been the first and killing shot! **RL**

Appendix 1
Examining horns to find the best areas for trophy hunting

Animals grow horns according to two factors. Firstly, the plan laid down in their genes for them to grow horns, and secondly, the nutrition available to them, enabling them to carry out that plan. It is often difficult to separate these two factors. Has an animal with short horns simply got a genetic plan for short horns, or was there was not enough food to grow horns to that animal's full potential? This question is particularly difficult to answer with deer. Stags cast their antlers each year and so there is little in the way of a history of horn growth for a hunter of wild deer to go by.

Chamois and tahr, in contrast, retain what horn they grow each year. As previously discussed, their horns grow in distinct annual rings. Thus they carry on their heads a year-by-year personal history record. Also, unlike most deer, the females of chamois and tahr grow horns. Thus both sexes can yield information to the inquiring hunter.

By examining horns, a hunter with a tape measure, a record-keeping system and an enquiring mind can build up a lot of valuable information. Perhaps the most useful sort of information is that which identifies those areas (valley systems, mountain ranges, etc.) most likely to hold animals growing particularly large horns.

As an example we will now examine the measurements of two buck chamois Roger shot in the same year but in different areas: the Godley River and the Two Thumbs Range. They were the same age and from 'permanent resident' type populations.

Annual increments of horn growth						
(average of the two horns, as measured on the front or leading edge)						
	Total length (mm)	Year				
		1	2	3	4	5
Godley buck	214	127	23	20	22	22
Two Thumbs buck	198	110	18	25	25	17

Examining these two sets of figures shows the following:

1. The buck shot in the Godley is 16 mm longer overall than the Two Thumbs buck. In the first year, the bigger Godley buck grew 17 mm more than the Two Thumbs buck. Thereafter the two bucks, on average, grew similar amounts of horn. Thus, the reason that the Godley buck has longer horns is because of the extra growth in its first year of life. This first year difference, like any particular year's horn growth, could be a result of either genetics or feed conditions.

Genes are acquired from one's parents. 'Permanent resident' chamois live in herds more or less geographically separated from one another, and so the different groups scarcely interbreed if at all. Therefore individuals in these herds may have minor characteristics in common that distinguish them from the individuals of other herds. (These variations between New Zealand herds are principally the result of the individual characteristics of the few animals that pioneered and settled each new area. The founding animals passed on their personal qualities to their descendants.)

Although the two bucks detailed above were shot in separate areas (and so from separate chamois herds), they were still taken from within the same climatic region of the South Island and in country of similar soil and vegetation. Thus we may assume food conditions would have been similar in that year for both the Godley and the Two Thumbs areas. Also the two areas have been colonized by chamois for about the same length of time. So the modification of the vegetation by chamois will have occurred at about the same rate. Again, we infer that the vegetation of the two areas provide similar nutrition for their animals.

From all this, we can conclude that the reason for the difference in horn growth in the first year of life is more likely to be genetics than feed conditions.

2. Considering the second, third, fourth and fifth years' growth. There are minor year-to-year variations between the two animals, but overall the average is similar. This is probably because the areas in which the two beasts were shot had similar climate and vegetation. This supports our conclusion that genetics is the key to that first year's significantly extra growth.

Thus if a hunter were to choose which area to concentrate his trophy hunting efforts in, the Two Thumbs area would be the logical choice on the basis of the examples given. Of course this is a very

Appendix 1

simplistic example. To be sure about conclusions such as these, one would need to build up large numbers of data sets from groups of animals from many different areas.

Our simple example is shown to indicate what is possible from an examination of the wonderful record that the rings on horns provide. We are not experts at maths; we simply directly compare sets of figures, as in the example above, bearing in mind where the animals came from, the year they were shot, and their sex. In addition to the measurements shown above, Roger often uses an additional measurement for each year's horn increment. He measures the diameter of the horn at the mid-point of each year's ring of growth. He then multiplies this diameter figure by the length of that ring. This gives a number that represents the 'total amount of horny material produced' that year.

We don't know of anyone who has exploited to the full the possibilities the annual rings provide. We haven't been able to find any published scientific evaluation of sets of such measurements of horns. There is undoubtedly a place for this. Hunters with computing or statistical interest may like to take up the opportunity.

Appendix 2
Ballistics for alpine hunters

The alpine hunter faces special problems when it comes to shooting both chamois and tahr with the same rifle. Chamois are small, thin-skinned beasts, whereas tahr are much larger and have a thick hide.

To make an informed choice of rifle calibre, bullet type and load, it is helpful to have a knowledge of the way bullets kill. There is a widespread myth that bullet velocity on its own has some magical 'knock-down' quality: that an animal can be hit anywhere by a high-velocity projectile and be killed. 'Even if it gets hit in the leg the shock will burst the blood vessels of the heart' — or somesuch. This is complete nonsense. Indeed, as we shall see, in certain circumstances a faster load will kill less efficiently.

Bullet placement

There are a number of factors that enable bullets to achieve a fast kill. First and foremost is bullet placement. We have already dealt with the best places to aim for deer in *Red Deer in New Zealand*; tahr and chamois have the same basic body design and the aiming points are the same. The function that the bullet (or arrow for that matter) performs is to bore a hole in the target, and correct placement means that the hole is bored in a vital part of the beast, killing it quickly.

Size of the hole

This is the second factor in securing a fast kill. Stated simply, a bigger hole has a better chance of covering a vital part and has a bigger effect on that part when it is hit. There are, as all hunters know, two ways of increasing the size of the hole. The first is by using a rifle of

Appendix 2

a bigger calibre, and thus a bigger bullet that makes a wider hole. The second is by making the bullet expand into a bigger diameter when it hits the target, i.e., by using bullets that mushroom on impact. This second choice is, however, not as simple as it sounds. As we shall see later in this section, the bullet still needs to penetrate the body of the animal to get into vital organs.

Amount of energy delivered

The third factor in securing a quick kill is the amount of energy the bullet dissipates when it strikes and penetrates the target. This is proportional to both the speed of the projectile and its velocity. Translating this into hunting terms, a light, high-velocity 6 mm bullet such as a .222 will have less energy available to use on a bull tahr than a heavy, high-velocity 8 mm bullet such as a .30/06. The light bullet may not even be able to get through the hide. The 'amount of hole' created by the .222 is therefore a lot less than the .30/06.

On the other hand, the .30/06 when used on smaller animals may go right through, leaving a clean surgical-type hole, and come out the other side with a lot of its energy still unused.

One way of avoiding this waste of energy is to use a bullet that expands more on impact, dissipating more energy inside the animal, making a bigger diameter hole and causing much more killing damage. This is an argument in favour of the 'mushrooming' bullets that is well known to anyone who reads hunting magazines, as the advertisers typically display pictures of their immaculately performing products. However, there are, unfortunately, two factors that make this much more complicated: bullet weight and speed.

Bullet weight and speed

The depth of penetration of the bullet into the carcass is related more to the weight of the bullet than its total energy (velocity times weight). For example, imagine a tahr struck by two bullets, each having the same striking energy but different weights. The first is lighter, with very high velocity, while the second is heavier and slower. The former is more likely to expand explosively within a few centimetres of the entry point and waste its energy in making a big shallow hole, like a crater on the moon, well above any of the deep vital spots. The heavy, slower projectile is likely to expand more slowly as it drills onward through the tissue, penetrating more deeply and killing more effectively. This difference applies even if the two bullets are made of the same metal and have the same shape. In other words, irrespective of their design, the weight of projectiles is the major factor influencing whether a wide, shallow hole or a deep, shallow hole is made.

Some conclusions

Bearing all this in mind, we can start to understand the problems that beset the alpine hunter. A specialist tahr hunter will look for a rifle that can kill efficiently at distance. As it is often difficult to judge the range when shooting across gullies, particularly in snowy conditions, this hunter may be tempted to choose a rifle calibre that has a higher velocity and therefore flatter trajectory — a .243, for example. But as we have just seen, the tahr's thicker hide means a heavy bullet is required — the very thing to cause even a .243 to have a more rounded trajectory.

To overcome these problems, some hunters try using different types of bullet. For example, hunters with high-velocity rifles using light bullets may choose harder, less readily expanding projectiles. However, the price they will pay is a smaller hole. On the other hand, hunters using larger-calibre rifles firing heavy projectiles that have no difficulty in penetrating the hide, can use a more rapidly expanding bullet to ensure the projectile stays in the animal and doesn't escape with some of its energy still unused.

When it comes to shooting lighter game such as chamois, the shooter using the high-velocity, lighter bullet will find that the harder projectiles suitable for tahr behave differently. They now go straight through the smaller-bodied animal and make a smaller hole as they go. It is therefore necessary to use more expansive bullets that use up their energy and make a bigger hole. Conversely, the slower, heavier bullets with more expansive tips will do excessive damage. The best option will most probably be a lighter bullet weight (flatter trajectory) plus a less expansive projectile. This combination will cause less meat damage and allow excess energy to be 'dumped' by the bullet exiting.

The final outcome will always be two different tools for killing what are two very different animals. If a single calibre is to be used,

Appendix 2

bullets with different characteristics will be needed for each animal. For the average New Zealand hunter this is the usual choice. Over the years, you can refine your loads. In particular, pay attention to the type of projectile you use. This is easier if careful post-mortem studies are carried out to study the behaviour of the bullets.

Alternatively, two different rifle calibres can be justified, but this leaves you with the disadvantage, according to which rifle is carried, of only being properly equipped to hunt either tahr or chamois, but not both.

Appendix 3
Wind chill

EQUIVALENT WIND CHILL TEMPERATURE °C

WIND SPEED — Kilometres per hour													WIND SPEED — Knots per hour
	70	-7	-14	-20	-27	-33	-40	-46	-52	-59	-65	-72	35
	60	-7	-13	-19	-26	-32	-39	-45	-51	-58	-64	-70	32
	50	-6	-12	-18	-25	-31	-37	-43	-49	-56	-62	-68	27
	40	-5	-11	-17	-23	-29	-35	-41	-47	-53	-59	-65	22
	30	-3	-8	-14	-20	-25	-31	-37	-43	-48	-54	-60	16
	20	0	-5	-10	-15	-21	-26	-31	-36	-42	-47	-52	11
	10	5	0	-4	-8	-13	-17	-22	-26	-31	-35	-40	5
	6	8	4	0	-4	-8	-12	-16	-20	-24	-28	-32	3
		8	4	0	-4	-8	-12	-16	-20	-24	-28	-32	

AIR TEMPERATURE °C

This chart serves only as a guide to the cooling effect of the wind on bare flesh when a person is first exposed. General body cooling and many other factors affect the risk of freezing injury. The equivalent wind chill temperatures used on this chart are based upon a neutral skin temperature of 33°C. With physical exertion, the body heat production rises, perspiration begins, and heat is removed from the body by vaporization. The body also loses heat through conduction to cold surfaces with which it is in contact and in breathing cold air that results in the loss of heat from the lungs. This chart, therefore, does not take into account all possible losses of body heat. It does, however, give a good measure of the convective cooling that is the major source of body heat loss. (Note: Wind speeds greater than 70 km/35 knots have little additional chilling effect.) Reproduced from the National Weather Service Wind Chill Chart supplied by the New Zealand Mountain Safety Council.

Appendix 4
Chamois usage of alpine zones

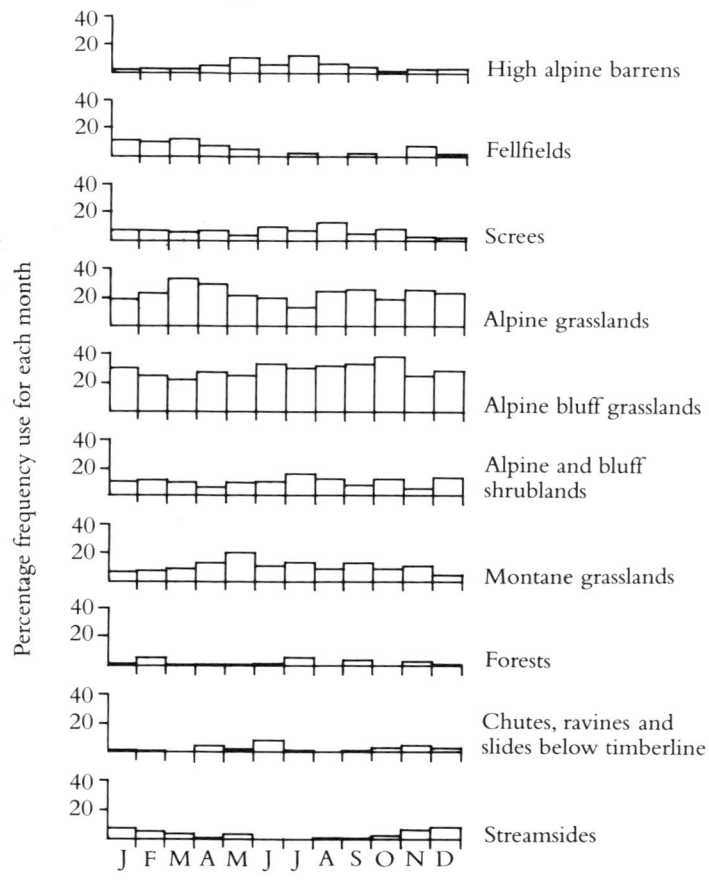

[Chart showing percentage frequency use for each month (J F M A M J J A S O N D), y-axis 0-40, for the following zones:]

- High alpine barrens
- Fellfields
- Screes
- Alpine grasslands
- Alpine bluff grasslands
- Alpine and bluff shrublands
- Montane grasslands
- Forests
- Chutes, ravines and slides below timberline
- Streamsides

Month by month use of various mountain regions by chamois in the Southern Alps. Reproduced from New Zealand Journal of Ecology *1986, Vol.13, page 194.*

Glossary

Altitudinal shift (as pertaining to feeding behaviour): Pattern of behaviour whereby animals move up and down the mountainside in response to the changing seasonal patterns of growth. Thus in spring they ascend the mountain progressively as the growth zone gradually moves up the mountain.

Annular rings: *See* Growth rings.

Barrens: Places where there is little fertility and thus little plant growth.

Body shake: Characteristic behaviour of rutting buck chamois in which the animal urinates at the same time as shaking his body, thus spraying urine droplets over the undersurface and sides of the body.

Bovids: Members of the ox family of ruminants, including cattle, sheep and antelopes as well as tahr and chamois.

Catabatic wind: Movement of air caused by changes in temperature brought about by the daily movement of the sun. At night there is a down-slope movement of cooler air whilst in the day there is an up-slope movement drawn by the rising of warmer air.

Carrying capacity: Maximum number of a species that can survive at equilibrium with the food supply in a given area. Numerically, at carrying capacity birth and juvenile survival rate equal death rate. When numbers rise higher food supply diminishes and death rate increases.

Cleaves: The two horn-clad, weight-bearing portions of the feet of deer and goats (ungulates).

Coat mismatch: Situation brought about by the fact that an animal was introduced to New Zealand having evolved for a different climate.

Glossary

This means that the animal may adapt its biological clock to our seasons, the winter coats are too warm, having evolved to cope with colder winters.

Diurnal activity: Animal behaviour where there is activity during the hours of daylight only.

Fellfield: Type of herbfield in which the plant community is more open. Generally found on more rocky ground.

Flash hider: A length of tubular metal added to the front of the barrel of the rifle. This is of larger diameter than the barrel and bears grooves along its length. This feature is useful to the alpine hunter in acting as a baffle against snow clogging. However, readers should be aware that under current legislation the addition of the flash hider to a semi-automatic rifle may lead the rifle to be classified as 'military style'.

Floater population: Biologists' term for a population of more mobile animals that builds up when all permanent residence sites are already in use by other members of the same species. If one of these latter members dies or otherwise vacates their site of occupancy the place may be taken by a member of the floater population.

Frost heave: Process whereby larger stones are gradually lifted out of the topsoil due to the action of frost.

Frostbite: A condition where the flesh becomes frozen due to cold. Commonest site is fingers and toes. The affected part becomes white and numb when cold, but is extremely painful when thawed out.

Genetic programme: Information that is carried in the animal's genes, inherited from the parents. It is not alterable by the influence of the environment.

Gestation period: Period of time from conception to birth, during which an animal develops within the womb or uterus.

Graupel: Mountaineer's name for snowflakes that have a well-rounded shape and are composed of more solid ice with little intervening air space. Similar to very small hailstones.

Growth rings: Tubular sections of horn laid down during one year. These are easily visible in tahr and common goats but more difficult to discern in New Zealand chamois.

Head-to-tail threat: Behaviour seen in chamois (and, less commonly, in tahr) when two usually juvenile animals stand parallel to each other or circle while in a head-to-tail position. Often there will only be posturing in this position but at times they have been observed to hook with their horns at their opponent's flank.

Head-shake: Behaviour of a rutting tahr bull, whereby he may interrupt his low-stretch behaviour and jerk his head down as if nodding, while at the same time shaking it from side to side.

Herbfields: A plant community found above the tussock grasslands and consisting of large herbaceous plants growing in abundance.

Herbs: Small plants, other than grasses, which have soft rather than woody tissues, and at the end of each growing season usually either die or lose their above-ground parts.

Herd: In the context of this book, a herd is taken solely to mean an assemblage of animals found in a given place at a given time, i.e., it is not used in the behavioural sense that implies some degree of interdependence of the members.

Hormone: Chemical signal from one part of a plant or animal to another part of itself. Generally, in animals the chemical is carried in the blood to the organ which it will affect. Thus in deer, hormones produced in the testicles of stags will be carried by the bloodstream to affect antler growth.

Horn: A permanent structure carried on the head by bovids. Horns grow on special extensions of the skull and have growth rings added each year. In comparison, antlers are temporary and shed each year.

Hypothermia: A medical condition in which an individual's body temperature drops below normal.

Kicking (in the context of mating behaviour): The name given to the males habit of momentarily lifting his foreleg as if to kick the female. In tahr this consists of lifting the foreleg some 15 cm off the ground and kicking limply with the leg slightly bent at the lower joint.

Lip curl: The behaviour of the rutting male in which the upper lip is raised and the nostrils simultaneously flared. The display is usually given when the male is endeavouring to detect a female's readiness for mating and is synonymous with 'showing flehmen'.

Low-stretch: A dominance and mating display commonly recorded in goat-like animals including chamois and tahr, in which the shoulders are humped and the head is held low with the neck almost parallel to the ground. The animal typically holds the head in a position with the chin elevated. In tahr the tail is often raised vertically at the same time.

Nilgiri tahr (*Hemitragus hylocrius*): A species of tahr, related to the Himalayan tahr, that lives in the high tablelands of Southern India known as the Western Ghats. The populations are found from 7-10 degrees north making them the worlds most equatorial wild goat-like animal.

Nocturnal activity: Activity during the hours of darkness.

Pizzle: Alternative term used by hunters for penis.

Post-cornual gland: Scent gland on the forehead of chamois, in the mid-line behind the base of the horns. This gland is active in the male during the rutting season, producing a musk used for scent marking.

Rumen analysis: The examination of the contents of the rumen in order to find out the identity of the plants that are being eaten.

Rumen: The large sac found at the start of the stomach of ruminant herbivores. It acts as a storage organ and fermenting chamber for plant food.

Ruminant: A sub-order (larger group than family) of hoofed, cud-chewing mammals including deer, buffalo, camel, giraffe, etc., as well as the bovids which include chamois and tahr.

Rutting pit: An excavation dug by American mountain goat males during the rutting season. It serves a similar purpose to the wallow made by male deer of some species.

Scree: Shingle fan in which the size of stones and angle enables a mountaineer to walk down it in safety.

Showing flehmen *See* Lip curl.

Silage: Partly decomposed, compressed remains of herbs and grasses eaten by herbivores.

Sluffing: A behaviour exhibited by snow where, as a consequence of poor adhesion between the particles, there is down-slope movement of small areas of the pack leaving a characteristic 'V' shaped signature on the snowfield. It may indicate a high probability of powder avalanche.

Tahr: In the context of this book this name refers only to the Himalayan tahr *(Hemitragus jemlahicus)*. There are in fact three species of tahr, the others being Nilgiri tahr *(Hemitragus hylocrius)* and the Arabian tahr *(Hemitragus jayakari)*. The word tahr is sometimes spelt thar, but the leading expert, George Schaller, considers this to be a mis-spelling.

Threat bounding: Aggressive behaviour exhibited by rival males in which one or both will rear momentarily on hind legs as if to lunge at the opponent in the manner of clashing bighorn sheep.

Tongue flicking: Behaviour sometimes added to head-shaking in the low stretch given by bull tahr when approaching a female that is in season. The tongue is flicked rapidly in and out of the mouth.

Trajectory: Path taken by the bullet from rifle to target.

Twisting (in the context of tahr rutting behaviour): Behaviour exhibited by the bull tahr when displaying at the low stretch (or head up). The head is turned to face away from the female so that the horns point away from her.

Bibliography

Anderson J. A., Henderson, J. B. (1961), "Himalayan Tahr in New Zealand", *Aspects of life history and assessment of management problems*, NZDA Special publication No. 2.
Briederman L. (1961), "Investigations in chamois in the Elbsahdstein district", *Zeitschrift fuer Jagdwissenschaft* Vol. 7 No. 4, 139-166.
Caughley, G. (1961), "Horn rings and tooth eruption as criteria of age in the Himalayan Tahr", *New Zealand Journal of Science,* 8: 333-351.
Caughley, G. (1970), "Habitat of Himalayan tahr", *Journal of the Bombay Natural History Society*, 76: 103-105.
Caughley, G. (1971), "The season of births for northern hemisphere ungulates in New Zealand", *Mammalia,* 25: 204-219.
Clarke, C. M. H. (1985), "The ecology of the chamois *Rupicapra* in an alpine basin in southern Nelson", Unpublished thesis, University of Canterbury.
Clarke C. M. H. (1986), "Chamois movements and habitat use in the Avoca River area, Canterbury, New Zealand", *New Zealand Journal of Zoology,* 13: 175-198.
Clarke C. M. H. (1978), "How far do chamois range (Basin Creek study area)?", *What's New in Forest Research* No.60.
Clarke C. M. H., Frampton C. M. (1991), "Structural changes in an apparently stable chamois population in Basin Creek, Canterbury, New Zealand", *New Zealand Journal of Zoology,* 18: 233-241.
Clarke C. M. H., Henderson, R. J. (1984), "Home range size and utilisation by chamois in the Southern Alps, New Zealand", *Acta. Zool. Fennica.* 171: 287-291.
Christie A. C. H. (1961), "A note on the chamois in New Zealand", *New Zealand Journal of Zoology,* 32-36.
Christie A. C. H. (1966), "The sensitivity of chamois and red deer to

temperature fluctuations", *New Zealand Journal of Zoology*, 1966 34-38.

Ferber, P. (1974), *Mountaineering, the Freedom of the Hills*, The Mountaineers Press, Seattle, Washington.

Henderson, R. J., Clarke, C. M. H. (1986), "Physical size, condition and demography of chamois in the Avoca River region, Canterbury, New Zealand", *New Zealand Journal of Zoology*, 13: 65-73.

Kramer, A. (1969), "Sociale Organisation und Sozialverhalten einer gemspopulation (*Rupicapra rupicapra*) der alpen Z", *Tierpsych*, 26: 899-964.

Lambert, R. E., Bathgate, L. L. (1977), "Determination of the plane of nutrition of chamois", *Proceedings of the New Zealand Ecological Society*, 24: 48-56.

Lovari, S. (1985), *The Biology and Management of Mountain Ungulates*, Croom Helm.

Parkes, J. P. (1993), "F.R.I. rumen studies of tahr and chamois".

Parkes, J. P., Tustin, K. G. A. (1985), "A reappraisal of the distribution and dispersal of female Himalayan Tahr in New Zealand", *New Zealand Journal of Ecology*, 8: 5-10.

Perla, R., Martinelli, M. (1976), *Avalanche Handbook*, US Dept. of Agriculture and Forest Service Handbook 489.

Pohle, H. (1944), "Hemitragus jemlihicus schaeferi", *Zool. Anzeigner* 155: 184-191.

Rice, C. G. (1988), "Reproductive biology of Nilgiri tahr (*Hemitragus hylocrius*)", *Journal of Zoology*, London, 214: 269-284.

Schafer, E. (1950), "Uber den Schapi (*Hemitragus jemlahicus schaeferi*)", *Zool. Anz.* 145: 247-260.

Schaller, G. B. (1973), "Observations on Himalayan tahr (*Hemitragus jemlihicus*)", *Journal of the Bombay Natural History Society*, 70: 1-24.

Schaller, G. B. (1977) *Mountain monarchs, wild sheep and goats of the Himalaya*, University of Chicago Press.

Schroder W. (1971), "Studies on the ecology of the chamois (*Rupicapra rupicapra*) in one region of the Alps where it occurs", *Zeitschrift fur Jagdwissenschaft*, 17:113-168.

Tustin, K. G., Challies, C. N. (1978), "The effects of hunting on the numbers and group sizes of Himalayan tahr in Carneys Creek, Rangitata Catchment", *New Zealand Journal of Ecology*, 1: 153-157.

Tustin, K. G., Parkes, J. P. (1988), "Daily movement of female and juvenile Himalayan tahr (*Hemitragus jemlihicus*) in the eastern Southern Alps in New Zealand", *New Zealand Journal of Ecology*, 2: 51-59.

Index

alpine barrens 64, 123
alpine clothing 37-8
alpine grasslands 65, 123
alpine scrubland 66
appetite regulation 87
avalanche 14-25, 83, 94
  avoiding 23
  classification 17-21
  fracture patterns 22
  helping someone caught 23
  if caught 21-3
  powder snow 17-18
  slab 19-21, 22, 24, 25
  wet-snow 18-19

balaclava 39
ballistics 43, 118-20
bedding areas 78, 94
binoculars 17, 43-5
body shake 72
boots 33-6

catabatic winds 25-6, 79
chamois
  anatomy 74-5
  calving 74
  coat mismatch 60-4
  competition other species 69-70
  diet 63-9
  field sign 78
  herd size 56
  horn growth 76-8, 115-7
  in mist 63
  in snow 61-2
  migrants 52-5, 70
  permanent residents 53-4, 70, 115, 116
  range and territory 51-5, 123
  rut behaviour 70-4
  senses 78-9
Chionocloa tussock 65, 69, 88
cornice 16
crampons 34-6
creeping cold 28
creeping matipo 66
creeping pohuehue 66

dish-leaved hebe 66
Dracophyllum 67, 90, 91, 100
dwarf bloom 88

Entrant 37

falling rocks 26
fellfields 65, 123
flash-hider 42
footfangs 34
frost bite 28
frost heave 26, 79

giant buttercup 88
gloves 38
Gore-Tex 37

head-shaking 97
hot-spot 66
hypothermia 27

ice-axe 36

kicking 97

lipcurl 97
long-johns 33, 37, 38
low-stretch 97, 98, 99

matagouri scrub 97, 90
Milair 37
montane grasslands 67, 123
mountain buttercup 65, 88
mountain daisy 56, 88
mountain gentium 66

pinatoro 66
poa tussock 65, 69, 88, 90
post-cornual gland 72, 75

red deer 111-2
rifle calibre 43, 118-20
rifle sling 37
rumen studies 88

scopes 42
  covers 42
  spotting 45
self arrest 36, 42
shingle fan 27, 123

showing flehmen 74
silver tussock 88
sling, rifle 39-40
sluffs 17, 18
snow berry 65, 88
snow deposition 16-17
snow gaiters 33, 34
snow totara 90
snowblindness 39
soil patch 72
storms 27-28
summer thermal cover 110
sunburn 39
synthetic rifle stock 41-42

tahr 82-103
  daily movements 84-6
  feeding 87-91
  forest dwelling 94
  horn growth 102-3, 115-7
  in bad weather 93
  overhang sheltering 93-4
  rut 94-9
  society 91-2
  spotting tips 99-101
tongue flicking 97
tricouni nails 34
Two Thumbs Range 101, 115, 116

wapiti 109-10
wapiti-red hybrid 110-1
willow herb 66
wind chill 27, 122